GRATEFUL RUNNING

MENTAL TRAINING FOR THE LONG DISTANCE RUNNER

BY

Dr. Grayson T. Kimball

Acknowledgements

I would like to give grateful recognition to the following people...

My wife Robin – my best friend, biggest supporter, and teammate for life, who now firmly believes in the power of positive thinking...some of the time.

My beautiful little daughter Scarlette Chayse – one day you and daddy will cross the finish line together.

My family – for continuing to support my running as only a Kimball can – with mockery and restrained praise.

Mom & Dad, Tracy, Rick, Emily & Michael, Tyler, Joyce, Bella, Miriam, & Zalman, E.J. & Alli, Spencer, Clayton, & Gram

Bubbles – this book began to materialize the day of the infamous 20-miler in March 2002; one of my worst runs ever and the pinnacle of your running career. Your loyalty and incessant willingness to always go above and beyond is truly appreciated. Here's hoping you have one more in you...you need it!

Jay – from our morning runs down Gibbs Road, to the road trip for the 2002 NYC marathon, to your continual opportune calls for mental guidance, you are responsible for initiating me into the world of marathon running and a primary reason why this book was able to come to fruition.

Alan Trist and Ice Nine Publishing – a very special thanks for generously granting permission to quote many of the lyrics throughout the book as a way of exploring the connection I have found between running a marathon and experiencing a Grateful Dead concert.

Chris DeFrancesco, alphabeticadesign.com – your imagination and creativity perfectly captured my vision for the book cover and gave this project its pulse.

Tim Weldon, weldoncreative.com - my editor, who did a fantastic job amending and revising the manuscript.

Dear Mr. Fantasy

Dedication

This book is dedicated to the memory of my grandparents –
Edward & Marion Kimball and George T. Klein

CONTENTS

PRELUDE TO A RUN

November 4, 2001
Boston, MA

"Once in a while you get shown the light in the strangest of places if you look at it right"

As a cool, brisk autumn breeze flows through my apartment window, I find myself spending a lazy Sunday afternoon listening to the soothing sounds of the Jerry Garcia Band and, curiously, thinking about the mental state of an educational sales consultant over 200 miles away. At this very moment, my long-time friend, Jay, is one of the 23,000 people putting themselves through the daunting physical and mental athletic challenge that is the New York City Marathon.

It's just after 4:00 p.m. when Jay calls to let me know he has finished the marathon. His only other marathon had been back in April 1999 when he ran the Boston Marathon in a most respectable time of 3:53:51. After taking a little over a year off from serious training, Jay was eager to jump back into the fray and train again. Motivation running high, Jay tossed his name into the NYC Marathon lottery and hit the jackpot – an official number! However, by the middle of September, both personal and professional issues had severely limited Jay's physical training regimen. Though his weekly runs were becoming less frequent, he was still convinced that he would compete in the marathon. It was at this moment that Jay realized he needed to add a whole new form of training in order to ready himself for the race.

Only a few months removed from my graduate program at Springfield College, I was just beginning to establish myself in the sport psychology field in Boston – a hotbed for everything that is running. Jay asked if I would teach him the mental training skills needed to prepare for the marathon. What could be better than having a good friend become your first client, right? So Jay and I devised a weekly schedule of sessions that included guided imagery, breathing techniques, thought recognition strategies and the development of positive affirmations to ensure an optimistic mindset for the final few weeks of training, as well as the 26.2 miles he would soon be running.

My last piece of advice to Jay was to develop a mantra that could serve as an instant confidence and energy booster any time during the race. Jay heeded my advice and maintained an inner dialogue that was simple and straightforward – "With every breath I take, I get stronger." What made this affirmation so effective for Jay was his belief that he was truly running stronger with each breath he took. By believing in himself and in the power of his mind, Jay ran a personal best 3:34:42 in the 2001 NYC Marathon (and followed that up with another personal best in 2002, finishing in 3:24:50). What was even more remarkable than his time was his post-race comment that there was no way he could have run so well and completed that race without the proper *mental* training routine. My first client, my first success.

A few weeks later, I received a call from another long-time friend, Ken (affectionately known as Bubbles to his closest buddies). Bubbles lived out in Chicago but was originally from the Boston area. He called to tell me that he had spoken to Jay about his sensational performance in the NYC Marathon, and how motivating it was to hear about the experience. A spirited and gregarious person to begin with, Bubbles had an added hint of excitement in his voice. I sensed he had some ill-conceived, impulsive idea formulating in his mind, which was not uncommon by any stretch of the imagination. His ensuing proposition changed my life.

As is his style, Bubbles unflinchingly declared, "I want to run the Boston Marathon this year, and I want you to run it with me." I'd expected him to ask for my help with his training, but running it with him? For a brief moment my mind went blank and I was at a loss for words. I had always thought about running a marathon but never took the thought entirely seriously. Then, in a moment of clarity, I stared out my bedroom window and visualized myself running down Beacon Street, which covers miles 22-25 of the marathon. What better way to immerse myself into my new hometown of Boston than by running the marathon. My response was pithy – "I'm in."

Just like that, the commitment was made to train for and run the most prestigious and challenging marathon of them all, the Boston Marathon. I was primed and ready to become part of an exclusive group – the less than 1% of the American population that has run 26.2 miles.

INTRODUCTION

Over the past decade, there has been a marked increase in the number of recreational athletes training for and running marathons. There are numerous books that outline physical and nutritional training plans for runners. While these books are great resources for a novice runner looking for some direction on how to get started or an experienced runner seeking to shave valuable minutes off his/her finishing time, they fail to give adequate attention to the most important aspect of training – mental training. Runners can successfully follow the most detailed physical training regimen and eat the most energy producing, muscle-replenishing foods. But if they do not have the proper mindset to cope with injuries, setbacks, nerves and self-doubt, then their training will go for naught. Runners need to learn to run with their heads and not so much with their legs.

Grateful Running is the only book that devotes itself entirely to the mental side of the marathon. This book has been written for all those people who have always wanted to run a marathon but never thought they could, as well as runners who are looking for ways to improve their marathon performance. I provide runners with practical and specific strategies to train their brain for success when preparing for a marathon. And unlike a textbook that delves into the theoretical explanations behind psychological constructs, this book takes a functional and concrete approach to understanding sport psychology. The applied concepts and strategies are presented in a succinct, distinctive and tangible manner that is easy to grasp.

As soon as someone finds out that my profession is sport psychology consulting, they seem both oddly fascinated and curiously perplexed. When referring to my work, the most common response I hear is, "Wow, that's pretty cool, but what exactly do you do?" I would not be surprised if you're thinking the same thing. What exactly is sport psychology and how can it help you? Without boring you to death with scientific, textbook definitions, I'll make it as simple as possible.

Sport psychology can be summed up in the following three words:

1. Thoughts➜ 2. Feelings➜ 3. Performance

These three words can change the way you run! As a runner, you need to understand that it is your thoughts and feelings that will influence your performance. The way you think affects the way you feel and the way you feel can impact how you perform. Your performance, in turn, can then influence your thoughts and feelings for your subsequent run. Yes, you need to have an adequate level of endurance to make it through your runs, but your success is not directly linked to your physical attributes. In fact, many of the day-to-day variations in our performance stem from mental limitations, not physical limitations. This just accentuates the importance of having the skill set to deal with the issues and adversity that are bound to arise in your head. By learning how to identify and, when necessary, adjust your thoughts, you will improve how you feel and ultimately gain control over your athletic and personal performance. Therefore, it is my job to make sure that everything happening from the neck up in an athlete is functioning properly.

"I'm too old, I'm too slow, I'm too fat, I've never been a runner, I don't have time"…these are typical excuses that follow the familiar decree – "I want to run a marathon, but…" True, running a marathon can be an intimidating venture into the unknown, but it can also serve as a catalyst to help you achieve life-long goals you once thought were unachievable. After finishing a marathon, people begin to think they can accomplish virtually anything they put their mind to. Having the proper mindset in sport and life can be the distinguishing factor between success and failure. When it comes to marathon training, your mind can be your best friend or your worst enemy. Developing mental toughness as a runner will help keep your emotions in check, allowing you to sustain your responsiveness, strength and resiliency when faced with competitive stress, challenges and pressure. An added bonus of this book is that the topics, techniques and strategies are applicable to everyday situations, and can help prepare you not only for a triumphant marathon, but for a thriving and engaging life.

Having run six marathons, I am a firm believer that distance running is 90% mental and 10% physical. You don't have to be an elite athlete, run six days per week and carry less than 4 ounces of body fat to run a marathon. Once your body gets used to the normal rigors of running, it is your mind that carries you the rest of the way. Having coached and consulted with hundreds of marathon runners, I have a delicate awareness of the natural trepidation and angst a runner faces when they begin this exciting journey. The vast majority of these runners are just like you. They are recreational runners, hold a regular job, have a social life, some are single, some are married and some have kids. The point is that they all find a way to balance their personal and professional lives, and find the time to challenge themselves to achieve one of the greatest athletic accomplishments in the world.

Two of my passions in life are running and music. This book has allowed me to combine them both in an innovative and enjoyable manner. Many runners get pleasure from running to music as it can instantaneously enrich their mood and turn a boring, painful, uneventful run into a surreal experience in which they enter the proverbial 'zone.' Every runner has his/her favorite musician or song they turn to for motivation. From my experiences, no other band offers such subtle words of inspiration and so clearly captures 'the moment' quite like the Grateful Dead. That is why you'll find passages from their songs pertinently sprinkled throughout this book. Whether or not you're a Deadhead, I'm confident that you'll come to appreciate their prudent words over the course of our journey.

So as Jerry Garcia so fittingly sang…*Long distance runner, what are you standing there for? Get up, get out, get out of the door…*

SET I: PREPARING FOR SUCCESS

CONCEPTS AND STRATEGIES TO DEVELOP THE MENTAL STRENGTH TO CONQUER 26.2 MILES

"FAILING TO PREPARE IS PREPARING TO FAIL."

These were the words of legendary UCLA basketball coach John Wooden. Coach Wooden was not referring to just the physical preparation of his players, he was also alluding to the mental preparation they had to put in on a daily basis to constantly perform at their highest level.

As a marathon runner, you will put in hundreds of hours of physical training. Having a solid base of physical strength and endurance is essential for all runners but it is only a fraction of the battle. Developing the mental toughness, strength and discipline to endure the peaks and valleys of training is what will get you to the finish line.

In this section you will learn how to self-motivate; set challenging yet realistic goals; overcome fears; maintain a positive mental attitude; visualize success; foster self-awareness; develop rituals and routines; enter the running zone; and remain calm, poised and focused during your marathon training and on marathon day.

In short, you will discover how to prepare for success.

CHAPTER 1: MOTIVATED TO ACHIEVE SUCCESS

"Inspiration, move me brightly"

When I made the conscious decision to run the Boston Marathon in 2002, there was no doubt in my mind that I would finish it. I had no idea how long it would take to finish the marathon or exactly what the training would entail, but I was convinced I could do it. This was not the first time the idea of running a marathon had crossed my mind. Back in August of 1999, along with a few friends from graduate school, a pact was made to train for and run the 2000 Boston Marathon. We would start training in November and keep in touch with each other on a weekly basis. It sounded great at the time…maybe because the idea happened to emerge toward the end of an evening littered with revelry and libations. But like many people who have had this grandiose idea, our goal of running the marathon fell far short of the finish line. I think it may have been about a month later when everyone bailed out – and we were still two months away from actually starting our training!

Training and running a marathon can be a positive, life-altering experience. It is not often that we choose to push ourselves past our perceived limitations, especially on a physical, mental and emotional level. Saying you want to run a marathon is one thing, actually going through with it is another story altogether.

Dedicating four to five months of your life to anything is not easy, let alone the uncertainty of doing something you may have never done before. It takes a lasting commitment to get up at 6:00 on a weekend morning and run 17 miles. Depending on the marathon you plan to run and where you live, you may be running in 85-degree heat or frigid temperatures in the single digits. A mentally tough runner, which you will become, is able to put the elements, distractions and self-doubt aside and focus on the task at hand. Having the desire to achieve a level of success that truly makes you feel good about yourself is how a mentally tough runner stays committed. In general, marathon runners tend to be the most motivated group of athletes in the world. Who else voluntarily wakes up at the crack of dawn on a bitter-cold winter morning to run 15 miles? Exactly!

People always talk about having to *find* the motivation to begin a task. Where do they plan to find this motivation? Is it under the sofa cushion? Is it behind the closet door? Where can a runner find motivation? If they look in the mirror, the proper motivation will be staring right back at them. Many runners neglect to understand that the belief in their ability to complete a task resides within them, not in some secret hiding spot. So before we futilely try to *find* the motivation to run a marathon, let's first get a clear understanding of motivation.

Many people vaguely define the term motivation and usually associate it strictly to a personality trait – "Johnny is a real self-starter." When someone negatively comments on our level of motivation, what do they mean by it? Are they implying we are apathetic? Are they implying we lack clear, specific goals? Ambiguous definitions of motivation only lead to confusion.

> **Motivation is a combination of our personality characteristics and our environment**

The healthiest way to view motivation is to interpret it as the direction and intensity of effort. Direction refers to the types of activities we choose to pursue while intensity refers to how much effort we put into that activity. Since you are reading this book, it is safe to assume that you have decided to direct your efforts into training for a marathon. The more important question, however, is how much effort will you put into your training? A runner's level of motivation is not simply the byproduct of their personality or the result of their environment. It is the interaction of the two. Your level of motivation to train for the marathon will emerge from who you are *and* where you are. The combination of your personality, goals and expectations, along with a positive and supportive training environment, will produce the ideal level of motivation.

One piece of advice I give to runners is to "Never disrespect the institute of the marathon." It is paramount to have a structured program to follow and to track your progress. Taking things one day at a time, seeing the little improvements we make day-to-day and week-to-week motivates us to work harder and eventually put ourselves in the best possible position to succeed. I have seen a number of runners cut corners in their training, believing that on race day they'll be able to 'turn it on' and finish. Many of these runners end up dropping out half way through the race due to poor training and conditioning, all stemming from a lack of commitment put forth on their behalf.

> **Our level of competitiveness will influence our choice of activity, intensity of effort, and persistence**

The reasons why people decide to run marathons are plenty. Some choose to run simply because they want to challenge themselves and see how far they can push their bodies. Others are trying to improve on a previous finishing time. These runners are intrinsically motivated, meaning they have the desire within themselves to get off the couch and begin training. Others may have an external reason for running, such as wanting to get in shape to look good for the summer, or their boyfriend/girlfriend wants them to do it, or they choose to raise money for a particular charity. While some people may need an impetus to get them started, relying too much on external motives for participation may eventually decrease motivation. There may come a point in time during your training when you ask yourself, "Why am I doing this?" And if you don't have a genuine and valid answer that may very well be your last training run.

> **A time will come when you need to want to achieve a level of success for your own self-worth**

A great example of how an external root can positively influence intrinsic motivation comes from the charity groups that I have coached. The people who sign up to run for a charity are raising money for a very worthwhile cause, most often for disease research. Many of the participants have a friend or family member battling the disease, or are survivors of the disease themselves. The majority of them are first time marathoners and some are first time runners! While the prospect of raising money for an incredible organization may be the incentive to begin training for a marathon, they do not view their participation solely for this reason. As they become more comfortable with running, I begin to see some of their internal competitiveness come to the forefront. They start challenging themselves to run more frequently and faster while persisting in difficult conditions. So while they may have needed the initial 'push' to get going, they were ultimately able to unlock their internal drive. For those who truly enjoy the experience, their running does not end at the finish line. They make running an essential part of their lives.

Since it is ill-advised to rely on someone else or some extrinsic reason to wholly facilitate motivation, it is critical to learn how to self-motivate. Personality factors can play a significant part in our ability to self-motivate. People who are generally seen as being 'high achievers' are confident in their abilities, rarely have thoughts of failure and constantly strive to achieve success. Further, they tend to seek out challenging situations and enjoy competing in these environments. Thus, a high achiever will certainly seek out a challenge such as a marathon and enjoy the process of training for and running the event.

On the other hand, 'low achievers' constantly have thoughts of doubt and seek to avoid failure. In this case, the thought of running a marathon may be floating in their mind, but the uncertainty about possible success will most likely deter them from following through on their idea to run.

A runner with a high level of competitiveness will push for excellence when they engage in an activity, and is bound to have greater motivation for that activity. Runners will choose to challenge themselves, train often, put forth maximum effort during training and persist in the face of adversity. Additionally, having a strong desire to strive for task success (like simply finishing a run as opposed to beating someone during that run) will allow a runner to experience a strong sense of pride in their accomplishments which can sustain their motivation.

> **High achievers strive for excellence, expect success, and experience pride in their accomplishments**

Another way to establish appropriate motivation for running is to have a sensible plan of attack. Runners need to take the time to map out the process of training for the marathon. Having a clearly-defined game plan, otherwise known as 'goal-setting,' can make all the difference in the world when you begin your training. Before you move on to the next chapter, take a moment and complete the following activity on the next page.

MENTAL STRONG RUNNING: STRATEGY #1

🏃 Runners are able to maintain a high level of motivation when they identify an internal reason for competing. Identify your true motives for wanting to run the marathon:

🏃 Describe your personality traits that will help you develop a high level of motivation and competitiveness:

🏃 Describe your training environment by identifying the situational factors that can help enhance your motivation:

🏃 Make the choice to think about how often and hard you are willing to work when engaged in training and how you plan to persist when things do not go your way:

CHAPTER 2: GOALS & EXPECTATIONS

"I told Althea I was feeling lost, lacking in some direction"

I was sitting at dinner with one of my clients, Todd, discussing his training plan for the 2006 Chicago Marathon. Ever since he had suffered and struggled through the intense heat and humidity of the 2005 Boston Marathon, Todd had been targeting this race as his redemption. He was very eager and motivated to begin, but somewhat lost as to how he was going to make it all happen. As Todd perused his training schedule, three things jumped off the page…the three 20-mile runs. Misery and consternation immediately crossed his face, a classic case of stressing too much about the future and not focusing on the present. Before I would let him get too worried about these twenty mile runs (which were still many weeks away), I told him to look at this program from a different perspective; a process vs. outcome perspective. Instead of being consumed with the mileage (the outcome of the program), he needed to remember that he wanted a program designed to make him faster and more efficient (the process of the program).

Todd had experience running marathons, so 'finishing' was not his primary concern. His sights were set on trying to set a personal record on a flat course during the pleasantly cool fall season. We created an individualized plan that was specifically tailored to both his physical and mental strengths and weaknesses. By having an actual plan, Todd was able to pay attention to details and monitor his progress on a daily and weekly basis. The simple mindset of 'process over outcome' allowed Todd to experience small successes throughout his training, which had a profound impact on his confidence.

Goal setting serves many important functions for runners. First and foremost, goals guide what runners do in both training and in the actual marathon. Goal setting also allows runners to properly plan on *how* to achieve specific objectives, which leads to enhanced feelings of organization and control in training and in their everyday lives. By conscientiously following a detailed plan, runners are far better prepared for every aspect of their upcoming runs.

> **Focus on the process of what you want to do rather than the outcome of what you hope to achieve**

Training for a marathon can be overwhelming for even the most organized runner, so it is of supreme importance to have a clear vision of how to achieve this task. When designed correctly, goal setting is an effective mental tool that runners use to increase motivation and confidence while simultaneously decreasing performance anxiety, burnout and boredom. If designed incorrectly, runners may experience a myriad of physical and psychological setbacks. The following are three common problems I have seen runners encounter when setting goals:

1. *Setting too many goals at once* – As marathon training begins, runners are likely to think about a multitude of things they would like to accomplish. In the instant gratification society we live in, runners want to achieve all of these goals immediately. Rome wasn't built in a day so do not expect all of your goals and expectations to happen at once. You have a solid 4-6 months of training, so be patient about what goals you would like to achieve and when you would like to achieve them.

2. *Setting goals that are way too general* – When I ask runners what their goals are for the day, I often hear the following: "To have a good run"…"To run my best today"…"To have fun when I am out there on the course." What do these goals mean? What is a 'good' run? What would constitute a runner running his/her 'best' today? What exactly is having 'fun' on the course? As you can see, the more general the goal, the harder it will be to know if you actually achieve it.

3. *Failing to adjust goals once they are set* – Goals are not written in stone, so take advantage of their flexibility. You are scheduled to run 15 miles today but you've been battling a cold all week. After a few miles you know you will be unable to complete the distance. Why kill yourself trying to finish? Simply adjust the goal and feel happy that you were able to run any mileage in light of your physical condition.

Too much angst about the future will only lead to further pressure and anxiety which can greatly inhibit and hinder performance. Breaking down workouts on a daily, weekly and monthly basis can help a runner focus on the small improvements that occur throughout training, and ultimately raise his/her confidence level for the more intense training down the road.

> *Challenging, yet realistic goals are a great way to boost motivation and keep you focused throughout training*

Before you head out for your first training run, take some time to research different marathon training programs that will serve as the foundation to your training. There are hundreds of programs available in books and online, so find the one that is best for you. I've found the book *Run Less, Run Faster* to be a great training resource for runners. The book's authors have created a revolutionary '3plus2' training regimen that is based on three quality runs (speed run, tempo run and long run) and two aerobic cross-training workouts. Thousands of runners, including your humble author, have achieved great success with this program. (For more information on the book and training program, visit www.furman.edu/first.)

A clearly-structured training plan is the first step in designing an effective goal setting program for your training. Many runners like to have their training schedule planned out months in advance so they can work it around travel, family or work commitments. This process allows runners to better cope with unexpected circumstances during their 4-6 months of training.

Regardless of the training program you choose, think of it more as a template rather than a do-or-die proposition. Although the training schedule is purely physical, runners have a much harder time dealing with the mental aspect of missing one of the sessions. Many runners become obsessed with their training and believe that one missed day will ruin everything up to and beyond that point in their training. While getting in your required runs is certainly essential, do not try to make up for lost time by doubling up your workouts. If you miss a day, do not stress over it. Simply move on to the next day. A runner once told me that after missing a long run over the weekend, he decided to run 11 miles the following Thursday PLUS his scheduled 12-mile run three days later. This of course is nuts. Unless you are a highly-trained, elite runner, there are few training programs that recommend doing such heavy mileage in such a short period of time. More is not always better when it comes to marathon training.

> **Identify potential roadblocks to your goals and develop proper coping strategies. Prepare for everything!**

Proper training will boost your confidence throughout your program, but the marathon itself can still elicit unnecessary worry. The thought of 26.2 miles can be very intimidating, especially if you happened to struggle through a 'pedestrian' 9-miler. Going back to our 'process over outcome' way of thinking can help runners mentally manage the high mileage. Think of your upcoming 15-mile run as three 5-mile runs. By breaking down your run into smaller distances, the training becomes more manageable. How many times have you successfully run five miles? Probably dozens or even hundreds of times. So instead of working yourself into an outcome-oriented frenzy prior to your training run, choose to view it in a more positive and attainable manner. It is common for runners to view the marathon in five 5-mile segments, with the last mile as 'the bonus.' Some runners see it as three distinct parts – the first 10 miles, the second 10 miles, and the last 6 miles. Some even break it down into a two-part race – the first 20 miles and the final 6 miles. As you progress through your training, you will develop your own view on how to successfully manage the marathon.

The following 10 guidelines can help you develop a successful goal setting program and achieve peak performance on training runs and race day:

#1: Develop a mission or overall purpose for running – Why are you deciding to train and run this particular race? What is truly driving you to dedicate your time and efforts? Defining your reasons for why you are doing what you're doing will help give you a clear picture of what you are trying to accomplish. Is the overall purpose to simply run a marathon? Is it to raise money for a charity? Is it to run in memory of a loved one? Constantly reminding yourself of why you are running can serve as a motivational boost, especially during the dog days of training.

#2: Performance & process before outcome – First-time runners should focus on their performance (a specific standard usually compared to a previous performance) and the process of running (focusing on the details of what must be done to run well) as opposed to the outcomes (trying to finish in a particular time). If you ran two miles today, your performance goal could be to run three miles tomorrow. In this case, you are setting a performance standard against yourself. A process goal could be to keep your body leaning slightly forward during your run. This illustrates the process or the small details of what you need to do to have a successful run. Runners will begin to stumble upon roadblocks when they focus too much on the outcome of their runs. Becoming so focused on the time it takes you to run can actually take the enjoyment out of the training. However, as you gain more experience in your training and racing, it is then advisable to slightly shift your focus to a combination of performance, process and outcome goals. For example, you may set a goal to finish in the top 50 and improve on your time from the previous race.

#3: Set both long- and short-term goals – While it is important to know what you want to achieve down the road (complete the marathon), you need to set daily, weekly and monthly short-term goals to help you get to the finish line. Short-term goals allow you to achieve steady success. By knowing what it is you need to do each day for your training, you can reap the benefits of feeling good about yourself through your daily successes. If the goal today is to run three miles and you do it, you have achieved a new level of success today – which will boost motivation for tomorrow.

#4: Set challenging yet realistic goals – Challenging yet realistic goals ensure that you are pushing yourself slightly beyond your limits, but within the realm of your abilities. By setting unrealistic goals you are dooming yourself to failure, which can have an adverse effect on your motivation and confidence. Saying you are going to run five days a week when you haven't been running at all is a classic example of a novice runner biting off more than they can chew and trying to do too much too soon.

#5: Visualize yourself accomplishing your goals – The more we can see ourselves reaching a particular goal, the more likely we'll believe we can actually achieve it. Seeing success throughout training can lead to increased confidence in achieving success during the marathon.

#6: State your goals in a positive manner – Positively stated goals such as "I am going to have a strong run today" as opposed to negatively stated goals "I hope I don't cramp when running hills" illustrates a motivation to achieve success rather than a motive to avoid failure. Even though you "don't want to cramp" on your run, the simple act of making that statement can cause your mind to picture you cramping on the run. This, in turn, can cause the body to inadvertently trigger a cramp while running. Remember, positive thoughts + positive feelings = positive performance.

#7: Provide yourself with a support system – Take advantage of the people around you. Share your experiences with your friends, family, co-workers or other runners, as they may give you much-needed guidance, encouragement and support.

*#8: **Write your goals down** –* Ink it, don't think it. You are more likely to remember what you set out to do if you write it down. I cannot stress the importance of printing out your entire marathon training program before you begin training so that you will know the plan and can always refer back to it. With everything else you have going on in your life, the last thing you need to remember is how many miles you are supposed to run this weekend.

*#9: **Set flexible goals** –* Believe it or not, life can get in the way of your marathon training. So you need to be able to go with the flow. Depending on a number of circumstances your goals may change, so be flexible with them. Failing at a goal is not failing as a person. Many runners will set out with the goal to run a personal best but due to weather conditions, injuries or other unforeseen circumstances, they modify the goal to the situation. One particular runner I was working with had set a goal to finish his marathon in four hours. As he approached the halfway mark, he realized that four hours was next to impossible, so he modified his goal to 4:15. By mile 20 he realized that wasn't going to happen and changed his goal to 4:30. At mile 24 he accepted the fact that a 4:30 finish would not be a reality so he altered his goal once again to 4:40. When he crossed the finish line at 4:38, he truly felt a sense of accomplishment for being able to complete the race just under his newly adjusted goal time.

*#10: **Prepare for the problems** –* Mental planning can play a significant role not just in preparation for training runs and the marathon, but in how a runner *reacts to situations* during training runs and the marathon. Every runner strives to have an enjoyable and successful training run or race. Reality, however, tells us that problems will pop up. Take the case of Charlie, for example…

Charlie was training for his first marathon and felt like he was doing all the right things to ensure a triumphant race. He was following his schedule faithfully by logging the prescribed mileage, eating the right foods and taking a day or two off each week to physically recoup. He appeared to be doing everything according to plan – everything except preparing for a runner's worst enemy, Mother

Nature! Any time she unleashed her fury on a day he was scheduled to run, Charlie was quick to complete his run indoors on the treadmill. His dream of running a marathon was quickly going to turn into a nightmare. As luck would have it, the day of the marathon called for rain. Running 26.2 miles in the rain is far from ideal. Difficult? Yes. But not impossible.

Since Charlie had not trained under these conditions, he was ill-prepared for the big day. Anything that could have gone wrong for him did. For starters, Charlie did not know how to properly dress for the inclement weather. Instead of wearing an old pair of sneakers or waterproof boots on his way to the race, he wore his marathon sneakers. Not a good idea. By the time the race started, his sneakers were completely soaked. He also failed to bring a hat to run in during the race. Running a marathon is difficult. Running a marathon in the rain is even more difficult. Trying to run a marathon with rain hitting you squarely in the face is just pure torture. And even though his friends were planning to see him at the halfway point, Charlie did not even think to have someone bring him a dry shirt or an extra pair of socks to change into. Needless to say, Charlie experienced a level of stress all runners try to avoid by any means possible. His marathon ended at Mile 15.

The thought of running high mileage in the cold rain and snow *does not* invoke images of a peaceful, relaxing run. Why would it? Who would actually choose to run in those conditions? Mentally strong runners are the ones that choose to train in these conditions. Every time they run in less-than-ideal conditions, they develop mental toughness. Every time they do something an average runner wouldn't do, they develop mental toughness. Every time they prove to themselves that they can succeed under any and all conditions, they are developing the mental toughness needed to complete the marathon. They have learned to put their mind and body at peace during a brutal run. By preparing for potential problems, they have learned to accept and cope with adversity by convincing themselves that each of those difficult runs only makes them stronger mentally.

Some of the problems runners encounter may be environmental (bad weather or a tough course), some may be physical (fatigue, cramping, inadequate fitness), and some may be more cognitive or emotional (distorted thoughts and feelings about your running capabilities). Developing strategies to help cope with the adverse situations you have faced during your training runs will help in handling these challenges should they surface during the marathon. Proper coping tactics for physical and mental adversity allows runners to:

♦ Remain positive when struggling on a run

♦ Remain focused when struggling on a run

♦ Bounce back from struggles during a run

♦ Bounce back after poor runs and setbacks

♦ Remain calm & poised

♦ Handle distractions

♦ Gain a sense of control over their performance

Goal setting is only effective if it is actually implemented. Like many of the mental skills discussed throughout this book, it is usually easier to talk about them than to actually practice them. A great way to develop your mental toughness is to make it a point to identify your daily and weekly goals. Are you mentally strong enough to find a few minutes and think about what you want to accomplish for the coming week? ***Appendix A (Weekly Goal-Setting Sheets)*** in the back of this book provides you with the opportunity to proactively make yourself a better and more disciplined runner and person.

MENTALLY STRONG RUNNING: STRATEGY #2

Identify a few problems that occurred during your runs, or problems that have the potential to occur, and identify a coping strategy for each problem:

Example:

Roadblock: Feeling fatigued towards the end of a 5-mile run
Coping Strategy: Bring jellybeans for extra energy

Roadblock #1:

Coping Strategy:

Roadblock #2:

Coping Strategy:

At this point you have probably identified some of your desires and motivations to train, and have begun the process of structuring your 4-6 months of training. But runners beware: An inevitable sense of panic may pop into your mind. Fear not, however, as this is a common concern for many runners that can easily be overcome with the right mental training program.

CHAPTER 3: BEYOND THE COMFORT ZONE

"There's a fear down here we can't forget, hasn't got a name just yet"

A client of mine had come within minutes of a qualifying time while running the 2005 Boston Marathon. Like many runners who come so close to qualifying, the goal for the next marathon becomes quite clear – qualify! So, if my client wanted to get faster and shave valuable minutes off his time, he needed to incorporate speed training into his workouts. Speed work can be intimidating to some runners as it conjures up images of vomit-inducing, exhausting, full-blown, all-out sprints around a track. In reality, speed workouts are an extremely advantageous and challenging alternative to the customary and sometimes bland 4-5 mile daily run. They enable you to run faster with less effort during your daily training runs, which translates into improved race performances.

After I explained the benefits of speed training to him, my client was eager to begin. We outlined a game plan that would allow him to take a few months off to recover from the Boston Marathon before beginning to train for the Boston Athletic Association Half-Marathon, which was to be held in October. From my perspective, the ultimate goal was to have him doing speed workouts once a week during the half-marathon training. The immediate benefit would be a faster time in the half-marathon, but the long-term benefit would be the experience and confidence to incorporate speed workouts into his training for the 2006 Boston Marathon.

A few weeks passed and I checked in to see how the track workouts were coming along. His answer was a little surprising to me – "I haven't done any yet." Rather than push the issue, I simply reminded him about the importance of speed work to improve his training. A few more weeks went by and I asked again about the speed work. This time, the answer was a little more revealing – "I didn't have time to do the track workout today so I just ran six miles." This was a little disconcerting to me. Speed workouts are short, intense sessions. They typically consist of a 1-2 mile warm-up, approximately 2-3 miles of actual speed training on the track, and a 1-mile cool-down. The actual time of running is less than the time it would take him to run six miles. The response of "I didn't have time" didn't really make sense.

This was not a case of being strapped for time; it was a case of choosing not to engage in something different from his norm. Running six miles has never been a problem for him; improving his speed was the issue. In essence, he was making a conscious choice to *not improve* his performance. Now, there is nothing wrong with that decision. But if you truly want to push yourself to the next level, you cannot allow your competitive fears to prevent you from reaching your true potential. Consistent improvement happens only when we choose to challenge ourselves and push beyond our comfort zone.

> *The anxiety we feel from avoiding situations is often greater than the anxiety we feel when actually performing something different and challenging*

Every runner has strengths and weaknesses that they bring to the table. Common sense tells us that most runners, and people in general, would prefer to focus on their strengths rather than dwell on what holds them back. After all, who wants to spend time thinking about their faults? However, you would be surprised to find out just how many people could talk for hours about what they cannot do as opposed to what they can do. Think about a time when you have not performed up to your capabilities. Chances are you ruminated for hours about how you struggled. And while these limiting beliefs or fears about your ability to succeed as a runner can become quite difficult to overcome, you are actually doing yourself a favor. Identifying what may be holding you back is the key to improvement. Use the 'AAA' approach to overcome your fears:

Acknowledge, Accept, Attack

In order to achieve a higher level of performance, we must learn to take risks and face our fears. Doing what is comfortable and familiar is common for many of us. But too much of the same thing makes it difficult to improve. Runners will find minimal gains in performance if they continually train the same way.

> **The process of simply taking risks or chances is just as important as the outcome associated with the risk**

One reason for staying in our comfort zone is that we often have a perceived fear of our lack of ability to succeed at something new or difficult. It is not uncommon for first-time marathoners to be fearful of the training itself, the ever-increasing distances to run, unpleasant weather conditions, getting injured, or not living up to the expectations of others. Even experienced runners may have competitive fears – a more intense training regimen, failure to decrease their time, or an inability to place higher in a race.

Creating success in all areas of our life requires us to move toward our fears rather than avoid them. The more open you are to embracing and acknowledging your fears, the less they will intimidate you. If you continually push them aside these fears will fester and cause superfluous performance anxiety. As my coaching mentor, Rick Muhr, likes to tell his runners: "You need to get comfortable with being uncomfortable."

For many runners, the thought of the marathon can bring out limiting beliefs and fears. The main reason why this happens is the lack of pressure many runners experience during shorter training runs as opposed to high-mileage training runs or races. I have seen many runners run in a loose, relaxed and calm manner and then suddenly tighten up when the pressure is on to perform for real. You cannot replicate marathon-day pressure in training runs but you can always train with a fearless and confident attitude. Taking the same approach to the marathon as you do for your some of your training runs is a choice. Both the practice and competitive environments can be one in the same if you choose to view them as one in the same.

> **The real success or personal growth comes from what we learn as opposed to what we achieve**

Developing a positive mindset can help you overcome your competitive fears, move beyond your comfort zone, and help you release your mind from any perceived limitations.

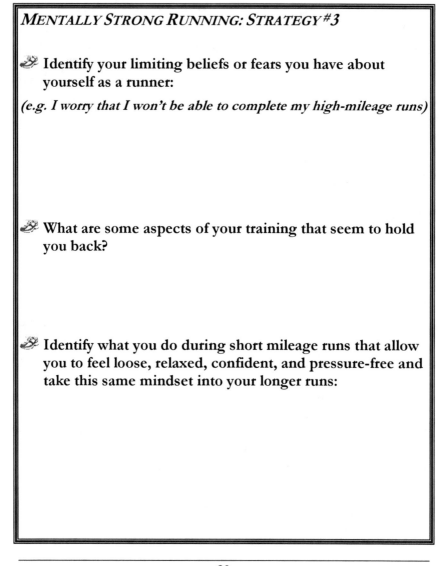

MENTALLY STRONG RUNNING: STRATEGY #3

Identify your limiting beliefs or fears you have about yourself as a runner:

(e.g. I worry that I won't be able to complete my high-mileage runs)

What are some aspects of your training that seem to hold you back?

Identify what you do during short mileage runs that allow you to feel loose, relaxed, confident, and pressure-free and take this same mindset into your longer runs:

CHAPTER 4: POSITIVE MENTAL ATTITUDE

"Dear Mr. Fantasy play us a tune, something to make us all happy"

My client, Brent, was training for his first marathon and embarked on his maiden run. The distance for that very first run was three miles. About halfway through the run, Brent had to stop and walk about a quarter mile. The remainder of that run was a combination of running and walking. The "G-rated" version of his reaction after finishing his run was, "I can't believe I couldn't even run three miles. How in the world am I ever going to run 26? There is no way I'm going to be able to do this." Well, with that attitude, he would have no chance to complete the marathon.

Unaware of his thoughts and reactions, Brent was creating a very common self-fulfilling prophecy – the negative prophecy – that is a mental barrier in which an expectation of failure actually causes failure to happen. This is a prevalent mindset because as a society we tend to think worst-case scenario more than best case. But when we can create a positive self-fulfilling prophecy – in which believing we can accomplish something actually causes success – we unleash the perceived limitations from our mind and body.

Prior to 1954 no runner had ever broken the 4-minute mile. In that year, Roger Bannister became the first runner to achieve this milestone. While his accomplishment is certainly remarkable, what followed may be even more impressive. In the year following his achievement, more than a dozen runners broke the 4-minute mile! How did this happen? Did runners radically change their training styles and miraculously become faster in one year? Of course not. The answer is quite simple – the impossible suddenly became possible. Think about it. No runner had been able to break a 4-minute mile, so it must be impossible, right? Wrong! As soon as one person broke it, the limiting belief that runners had placed upon themselves was now gone. If Roger could do it, other runners believed they could do it as well.

Back to our friend Brent. Fast forward four months after that initial humbling run, and Brent was crossing the finish line of the Boston Marathon. How did he make this happen? How was he able to change his outlook on his ability to run a marathon? The power of positive suggestion and a simple change of attitude, that's how.

Attitude will define your success when training for a marathon. If training were easy, everyone would do it. But it is not easy. It takes a positive mental attitude to deal with the failures, setbacks or misfortunes that may come your way. You will enjoy many fabulous runs that will make the grueling feel viable, but there will be some days when the elements will be working against you and make the demanding seem impossible. It is during theses times of struggle where you will make the most progress. When facing adversity or hardship, most people get angry and give into negative or frustrated feelings. This is a normal and natural response. It is very easy to think or feel this way due to the lack of enjoyment or success you may be experiencing. Effectively managing and controlling emotions during training runs and the marathon separates the successful runners from the not-so-successful runners. So you must learn and practice how to remain positive and optimistic no matter how tiring, demanding and challenging the task may seem.

> *The power of positive suggestion frees our mind of limitations and leads to high confidence and optimism*

Learning how to express your anger and frustration is very important, as it can turn into an uncontrollable emotion that ruins your ability to concentrate and decreases your self-confidence. From a mental standpoint, remember that anger is one letter away from danger. The more frustrated you get, the closer you come to losing control over your performance. If you have had success handling your anger in the past, great! If you have not had success with managing your emotions, do not panic. This chapter will help you identify strategies to better handle your emotions.

MENTALLY TOUGH RUNNING: STRATEGY #4

What can cause you to become angry, negative, or frustrated during a run?

How have you dealt with these issues in the past?

Identify how you have displayed a lack of control over your anger or frustration in the past. This could be a physical or mental response:

Identify what it is that you do to positively cope with your emotions and continue doing it:

Developing a positive mental attitude begins when we differentiate between perception and reality. Our mind has the ability to distort the truth, which can severely impact how we perform.

The following 'distorted perceptions' are common for runners to have when preparing for a run or during the marathon itself:

- **All or nothing thinking** – if one thing goes wrong during your run, you start to fear the worst

- **Perfectionism** – if you do not have the 'perfect' run, you see yourself as a failure

- **Thoughts of future failure** – anticipation that things will turn out poorly before you even begin your run.

- **Blaming** – you find yourself attributing failures and setbacks to factors that are out of your control (i.e. weather)

- **Disqualify the positives** – the belief that positive outcomes are the result of luck or chance rather than your own ability.

While it's normal to have these thoughts, we must realize that these limiting beliefs can often set us back in our training. Runners need to recognize the distinction between our sometimes distorted perceptions and the actual reality of our abilities.

MENTALLY TOUGH RUNNING: STRATEGY #5

Identify your distorted perceptions about your abilities as a runner, the way you handle adversity, etc.

What is the REALITY of these distorted perceptions?

One of the most commonly-used mental skills that can assist you in developing and maintaining a positive mental attitude is the skill of 'self-talk.' Any time we speak to ourselves, we are utilizing self-talk. What we think and say to ourselves can affect the way we feel and have a direct impact (positively or negatively) on our performance. The more positive thoughts we have going into a training run or race, the better our chances are of having an enjoyable and positive experience.

This may seem easy on the surface, but take a moment to think about all the thoughts you have had throughout your day. I'm willing to bet that over half of your thoughts have been negative. What was your first thought when you woke up this morning? Were you happy to get up and go to work or were you avoiding the fact that you had to get out of bed? How was your drive to work? Did you encounter any traffic this morning that put some negative thoughts through your mind? Were you running late? Dreading a meeting with your boss?

Negative thinking is all too common in our society and it can really bring down your morale. The good news is that you can control whether or not you will have negative thoughts and feelings. Being stuck in traffic is not fun, but why get so angry over something you have no control over? Wishing you didn't have to travel for work would be great, but the reality is, you do. The point here is that we can take a situation and make it worse than it seems simply by foreshadowing 'what if' and 'worst-case' scenarios.

Runners typically engage in two types of self-talk:

1. **Positive/Instructional Self-Talk:** Words or phrases that offer encouragement, increase effort, provide energy, foster a positive attitude ("I can do this"…"I love these challenges"…etc); and focus on the technical or task-related aspects of running ("Keep the knees up"…"Take it slow on the downhill"…etc).

2. **Negative/Instructional Self-Talk:** Critical, harsh, counter-productive, anxiety-producing and self-demeaning statements that prevent us from reaching our potential ("I hate hills"…"I can't do this"…"It's too cold out"…etc) and performing a particular task ("I don't want to stop during my 8-miler today").

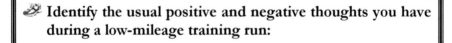

Mental strength is staying positive during times of struggle

What type of self-talk do you find yourself having when you are preparing for or are engaged in a run? Are you fearful of not being able to run the requisite distance for the day? Are you worried that the weather may not be ideal for the distance you are supposed to run? Are you thinking about not being able to finish your run and already getting psyched out for the long run next week? Or are you confident and ready for the challenge of running 10 miles in the rain? Remember, your thoughts and inner dialogue will dictate your success, so choose to think and speak positively to yourself!

MENTALLY TOUGH RUNNING: STRATEGY #6

Identify the usual positive and negative thoughts you have during a low-mileage training run:

Identify the usual positive and negative thoughts you have during a high-mileage training run:

The following three techniques are extremely helpful when trying to overcome a pessimistic attitude, manage your emotions, and maintain an optimistic and confident mindset.

1. **Thought Reframing**
2. **Thought Stopping**
3. **Positive Affirmations**

1. Thought Reframing

Identifying your thoughts is the first step in sustaining a positive mental attitude. Now that you have made a list of the thoughts that go through your mind when running and have categorized them as Positive or Negative, you are ready to start reframing the bad ones.

Once you are aware of the extent and content of your negative thoughts, you will need to counter or reframe them into positive, self-serving ones. What may seem like a harmless thought at first could really have negative consequences during a run. For example, thinking "I don't want to stop running for at least three miles" is a negative statement. Of course you don't want to stop running within the first three miles of your run, but you need to phrase this thought in a more positive light. The positive counter statement could be something along the lines of "I am going to make it through three miles and then assess how I'm feeling."

For every negative thought that pops into your head, you need to have a positive counter statement. Below are a few examples of common negative thoughts with a few positive counters.

Negative Thoughts:

♦ My body is so tired right now; there is no way I can run two more miles.

♦ It is so cold outside; this is the last thing I want to be doing.

♦ I hate running hills.

Positive Counters:

♦ Every new distance is a challenge and today is no different – step up to the challenge!

♦ It only takes a mile or two to warm up; I'll feel great after I finish this run so let's go!

♦ Every hill is a challenge and I love the challenge – I love hills!

Having these positive counter statements will prove to be beneficial if you choose to let them be beneficial. You must truly believe in what you are saying to yourself or these statements are nothing more than a fusion of meaningless words. Most runners will concur that running hills is not their favorite pastime. However, those training for the Boston Marathon have no choice as the course is littered with hills.

MENTALLY TOUGH RUNNING: STRATEGY #7

Looking back at your negative thoughts from Activity #6, reframe the thoughts by using positive counter statements:

Negative Thought:

Positive Counter:

Negative Thought:

Positive Counter:

Prior to a training run that included the famous 'Heartbreak Hills' in Newton, I asked the group of runners what their thoughts were about the numerous elevations they were going to face. It was unanimous – they were not looking forward to it. At this point, I explained to them the benefits of positive self-talk and thought reframing. They needed to restructure their internal dialogue to something far more positive and self-serving to help relax the mind and body. I told them to say "I love hills" as they approached each hill. Why? Because telling yourself that you love hills is the simplistic positive counter to "I hate hills" and it takes your mind off the act of running the hills. Well, the runners became more focused on saying the mantra than on the hills themselves. As the volunteers and coaches looked on, some runners were smiling, some were laughing, but all were saying "I love hills" – eliciting both a positive attitude and far more relaxed feelings as they made their way through the Newton hills.

2. Thought Stopping

Learning to manage negative thoughts as they occur and stopping them before they become detrimental to your performance is a critical skill to master. It is not uncommon for runners to find themselves thinking about poor past performances and setbacks, or experiencing excessive 'wishful thinking' during a run. Be aware of a negative thought as soon as it occurs and identify it as being harmful. Runners can make this a habit by periodically 'checking-in' with themselves throughout a run and asking the question – "What am I thinking about?" If the thought is positive, go with it and let it help promote peak performance. If the thought is negative, use an appropriate trigger word to actually stop the thought.

Many of the runners I've coached have learned a very simple, yet effective technique to stop the spiral of negative thoughts. They say or picture the word STOP when they realize they are being negative. It can be the sound of the word STOP or the image of a big red STOP sign that causes your mind to cease its negativity. This works well because we tend to associate the word STOP with the action of actually stopping whatever it is we are doing. So, just like you stop your car when you approach the STOP sign, stop your thoughts when they verge on negativity. Once the thought has been terminated replace it with a positive statement.

Another technique used to stop the stream of negative thoughts is called 'The Mental Trash Can.' If we have a material object that we no longer need or enjoy, what do we do? We rid ourselves of the item and throw it in the trash. Well, the same concept works when it comes to your thoughts. If you don't like what you are thinking about, take the thought and, in your mind, throw it into the mental trash can. Negativity is garbage so rid yourself of this waste. The more the trash piles up in your brain, the worse off you will be. Runners who practice and use this technique mention that they even hear the top of the trash can shut, abolishing the thought all together.

3. Positive Affirmations

During mile 25 of the 2002 Boston Marathon, I made a potentially grave mental mistake. With a little over a mile to go, I just wanted the experience to end. My body felt like it had been run over by a truck…twice. I was unequivocally enduring the greatest amount of physical pain in my life. The excruciating cramping in my calves, hamstrings, quads and groin is something I will never forget. In hindsight, I am pretty sure I could have crawled faster than I was running at that point. Be that as it may, I dragged my body around the final turn of the course onto Boylston Street; the finish line was in sight. My mantra was "Don't cramp, never again." Translation – as long as I don't cramp, I am NEVER doing this again. I could not have chosen a worse mantra to repeat. I actually felt myself cramp more and more every time I uttered that phrase. With a quarter mile to go, I realized my mistake and changed my mindset. I was able to put the day into perspective and think about the incredible accomplishment that was moments away. The euphoric experience of crossing the finish line erased all the physical pain and agony. As the finisher's medal was put around my neck, the mantra of "Don't cramp, never again" quickly turned to "I can't wait to do this again."

Positive affirmations and mantras are another way to confidently approach your performance and handle your emotions. They can be extremely helpful when your training conditions are predominantly difficult or you feel like you are struggling. Affirmations are nothing more than brief, meaningful, positive statements that focus on what you want to do or how you want to feel in a particular situation. This positive belief or thought is created to help you cope with a specific issue or deal with any stress you may experience while running.

As I mentioned in the prelude, Jay developed the affirmation of "With every breath I take, I get stronger." This statement served as a trigger for Jay to focus on his breathing and elicit the positive thought and feeling of running strong and confident. Jay repeated this mantra countless times throughout the final few miles of his race, especially when he felt like he was physically 'hitting the wall.' The result was Jay actually feeling his pace picking up...and achieving a personal best finishing time in the race. Eight years later, Jay continues to use that phrase for every race he runs. As you can ascertain from both my example and Jay's example, affirmations are personal, highly individual, and will probably have no relevance to others. Remember, this is all about you and what works for you and what will help put you in a positive mindset.

Here are some general examples that can help you maintain a positive mental attitude while running.

I believe in myself	*I am reaching my potential*
I am relaxed & calm	*I am focused & in control*
I get stronger with every step	*I let my performance happen*
I feel energized & confident	*I am a smooth & powerful runner*

Affirmations help you focus, keep you looking forward and enable you to handle unexpected circumstances

Guidelines for Creating Affirmations

♦ Writing your affirmations down will make the abstract more concrete. Some runners write their affirmations on post-it notes and put them in places where they will always see them (refrigerator door, screen saver, beside their bed, and even on their hand or arm while running).

♦ State affirmations in a positive light, as you do not want to steer your thoughts in a negative direction ("I don't want to cramp"). Focus on what you want to achieve and how you want to feel.

♦ Affirmations are more effective the more they are used. Saying something once will not create a magical sense of triumph. Build belief in your affirmations through daily repetition.

♦ The more concise and precise your affirmation is, the easier it will be for you to remember it. Keep in mind these are statements, not paragraphs. Too many words or ideas in a single affirmation will only lead to confusion.

♦ Affirmations should be stated in present tense since you are trying to improve performance at this particular moment. Affirmations that are directed to past or future feats can park your thoughts in the past or advance them into the future.

♦ Make your affirmations personal, dynamic and as powerful as possible by using words that are both inspiring and enlivening.

♦ Affirmations must be in the realm of your physical and mental capabilities. Unrealistic affirmations will limit your beliefs.

MENTALLY TOUGH RUNNING: STRATEGY #8

🐾 Develop your own positive triggers or affirmations to maintain your positive thinking:

Once you can monitor the content of your self-talk and maintain a combination of positive/instructional thoughts, you will find this to be an effective skill when you are out for a run and you need to control mental factors such as your attention or effort. Using trigger words like 'focus' or 'present' or 'right now' can help you effectively handle distractions and keep you in the moment. Phrases such as 'easy now' or 'push it' or 'keep the pace' can be beneficial if you feel your energy is low or you have too much adrenaline pumping.

One novice marathon runner told me that he could not run fast. He was able to ease his way into a decent pace but could never seem to get any faster. As his coach, I decided to put his mental strength to the test. During one of our long runs, I sidled up to him and asked him if he was at his typical pace. He said he was. I asked him if he thought he could run faster. He said he did not think so. I encouraged him to repeat the following mantra – "Run faster." As he started to utter those words, his pace actually picked up. I asked him to repeat this over and over until he approached the next water stop. He was amazed to learn that he actually ran a mile at a much quicker pace than he was accustomed to, thanks in large part to some simplistic, yet effective positive self-talk.

Developing and maintaining a positive mental attitude will also help you become a very confident runner. Sustaining self-confidence can be tricky. Many runners may find it easier to lose their confidence than to build their confidence. Your level of confidence, like everything else we have discussed, is completely within your control. Think about it. Why should a bad run destroy your confidence? Why should poor weather conditions destroy your confidence? The only way these events can ruin or diminish your confidence is if you let them.

A common belief about self-confidence is that setbacks will destroy confidence. This is total bunk – if you believe it is bunk! Mistakes and failures are part of life and part of running. It is during times of failure where learning happens. Runners can grow their confidence when they choose to focus on the small improvements and successes they have achieved, and then build on those positive experiences. Self-confidence stems from how we think, what we focus on, and how we react to our experiences. Positive thinking, focusing on factors within our control, and reacting positively to all experiences is what will build your confidence.

> **Runners with high confidence believe in themselves and use their mind to think about how they can be successful**

Runners can suffer from both a lack of confidence and over confidence. Runners who lack confidence tend to focus on their weaknesses rather than their strengths. Think of the last time you had an overall bad run. Did you dwell on what went wrong or did you think of some of the things you actually did well? Runners with a lack of self-confidence do possess the necessary skills to be successful but underperform due to their self-doubt.

On the other end of the spectrum are runners who are over confident. This type of runner has a false belief in their ability to succeed on a long run or in the marathon. Their confidence supersedes their actual running abilities. They typically suffer during their run as they don't prepare as well as they need to. They assume they can just show up and be successful. I have seen a fair share of runners put in a solid two to three months of training and then rest on their laurels. This usually translates into a miserable and dismal marathon experience.

Runners should strive to achieve an ideal level of self-confidence. This is a state of mind where a runner is fully aware of their physical limitations yet works as hard as they can to achieve their goals. Having this high level of confidence does not guarantee success, but it is essential for performing at your peak on a training run or on marathon day.

> *Self-confidence is the direct result of how we think, what we focus on, and how we react to adversity*

Tips for Building Optimal Self-Confidence

♦ Expect yourself to succeed. Always focus on your strengths and the great things you do as a runner. Never minimize what you do well. Once you begin neglecting the positive, confidence will suffer as your focus shifts to factors that cause you to struggle.

♦ If you have a setback or failure during training, view it as a learning experience. See it as a challenge and simply a stepping stone to future success. Focus on correcting any mistakes to prevent them from happening in the future. For example, if you failed to eat before your run and you felt tired just two miles in, make a note of that and know it will not happen again.

♦ Use imagery and goal-setting to boost your confidence. Seeing success and having a game plan will keep you on task and build self-assurance.

♦ Find items that symbolize your successes. Many runners have pictures of themselves at the finishing line or have a framed copy of their finisher's certificate hanging up in their room. These possessions can serve as a reminder of how you will continue to be successful in the future.

♦ Being in proper physical condition and feeling like you are well trained and prepared is another source of confidence for runners. You have probably taken some time to seek out the right training program for you. If followed properly, the 4-6 months of committed marathon training will have you physiologically and psychologically ready to handle 26.2 miles. Believe in your training.

♦ Environmental and situational comfort can build your confidence, too. Having the ability to run a race, even if it is half-marathon or 5-miler, will allow you to experience and become more comfortable in a race environment. Also, simply feeling like 'things are going your way' during a run can lead to situational contentment and ease any pre-existing anxiety.

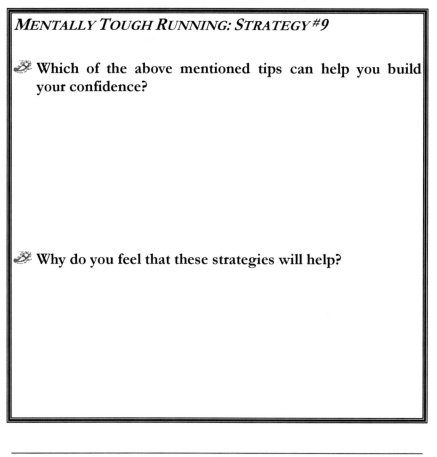

MENTALLY TOUGH RUNNING: STRATEGY #9

Which of the above mentioned tips can help you build your confidence?

Why do you feel that these strategies will help?

The principle of dominant thought states that "Whatever dominates my thoughts is what I move toward." By dominating your thoughts with success, you will continue to succeed. Therefore, it is imperative to keep negativity in its place. Once a runner begins to focus on a setback, they may very well perceive themselves to be a failure. The way a runner interprets this negative feedback will have an immense impact over the course of a training run or the marathon. If a runner has a poor start to a training run or for the marathon, they may be quick to infer a poor finish to that run. Do not sweat the small stuff and let it influence the big picture. There is always a solution to your problems. Learn from the mistakes that happen early in a run and figure out a way to fix them. Remember, your mind controls it all. You have the power to change your thoughts and focus on the positive aspects of everything you do. Running confidently and having a positive mental attitude will have an immeasurable influence on performance. To further facilitate this style of thinking, runners can learn to control their images and train their brain to see success.

CHAPTER 5: USING YOUR IMAGINATION

"Picture a bright blue ball just spinning, spinning free, it's dizzying with possibilities"

While you have been reading this book, chances are you have pictured yourself running. I'm pretty sure that you just pictured yourself running again after reading that last sentence. Every runner spends time visualizing an upcoming run, whether they realize it or not. Systematic imagery training can help improve your focus, build confidence, effectively maintain emotions, and even quicken the learning process of running-related techniques. The more you picture yourself performing a particular skill, the better you will be able to focus on that one particular skill and keep your mind 'in the moment.' The more you see yourself successfully running a certain distance or route, the more confident you will be when heading out for the actual run. The more you picture yourself maintaining composure during challenging times, the easier it will be for you to control your emotions during an actual crisis. The mental skill of imagery is the most widely practiced and most powerful skill an athlete can use to enhance performance. We all use imagery to either recreate or anticipate events due to our mind's ability to remember and create images. Think of your mind as a DVR. At any time, you can choose to recall or generate an athletic performance. Imagery serves as an additional form of training that occurs in our mind and will improve performance when practiced regularly.

Another benefit of visualization is that it can help runners prepare more completely and help them anticipate things more quickly when actually running. Before heading out for your training run, take the time to think about your goals and how you plan to achieve them. See it all in your mind before stepping foot on the road. When it comes time for the marathon, try to preview the course beforehand. Many of the websites are now providing visual tours of the racecourses. If you have the opportunity to actually drive the course prior to the race, take advantage of it. Knowing what is in store for you can help you develop a successful strategy of how you would like to run your race. Additionally, scouting the course can help you anticipate any potential problem areas and allow you to have a coping strategy firmly in place. When race day arrives, you want to feel as if you have already run the race – minus the cramping, dehydration and fatigue, of course.

As mentioned earlier, imagery is a powerful mental skill that can enhance performance and build confidence. This is the direct result of a runner visualizing successful images over and over again in their mind. Regardless of the skill or behavior you are trying to improve, the more you see yourself succeed in your mind, the more likely you are to succeed in real life.

While imagery can be a potent skill to boost performance, it also has the ability to impair performance if not used properly. Direct your thoughts to the following command – *"**Don't picture a baseball.**"*

Did you just picture a baseball? Chances are you did. Although you were instructed NOT to think of a baseball, you still did. Why did this happen? It's because the mind cannot differentiate between what's real and what's not real, between what's positive and what's negative. Your mind simply took the instruction to not picture something and actually pictured it. This is very similar to the self-fulfilling prophecy we discussed in Chapter 4 – expecting something to happen actually causes it to happen.

To effectively use imagery, you MUST keep your images positive. Always see yourself doing what you want to do as opposed to what you don't want to have happen. There is nothing wrong with picturing yourself correcting mistakes, but **do not** spend time thinking about the mistake. The more you think about failure, the greater the likelihood of failure happening again. If you are anticipating your upcoming 15-mile run and all you think about is the fatigue and exhaustion you may feel, you are setting yourself up for a distressing and arduous run. On the other hand, if you are visualizing yourself feeling stronger mile after mile, you are creating a positive image which can lead to an engaging and tranquil run.

> **Use the power of your mind to recreate past success or envision future accomplishments**

When my friend Jay was training for the 2001 New York City Marathon, imagery practice was a critical component in his overall training. I spent an hour every week with him developing proper visualization habits so he would feel as comfortable and prepared as possible to run his race. People in general, and runners in particular, hear the term imagery and often associate it with only one of our five senses: seeing. While it is common to only think of the 'visual' aspect of imagery, it is vital to incorporate all the five senses into your visualization practice. The inclusion of the senses allows the runner to make the imaginary experience seem as realistic as possible.

♦ What do you normally *see* on your run? Is it other runners, cars, a lake? Visualize the whole environment.

♦ What are the sounds you *hear*? Is it your music? Is it the conversation you have if running with a friend? Is it the sound of the cars, the birds, your breathing, or your feet hitting the pavement?

♦ When you are running on the road or a track, what does it *feel* like? How does your dri-fit shirt *feel* against your skin?

♦ How does your Mountain Blast Powerade *taste* after a steamy, humid run?

♦ On a warm summer day, can you *smell* the fresh-cut grass as you run down your street? Can you *smell* the exhaust of the cars passing you by?

While runners may personalize their imagery for an upcoming training run or race, the one common factor for every runner is that they must visualize the environment where they will be competing.

For example, it does not make much sense to visualize yourself running a flat course if the actual course is going to have hills. Visualizing your competitive environment can ease some of the angst of an upcoming run. The more you visualize yourself 'powering your way' up the hill, the more confident you'll be when you encounter the hill for real.

Additionally, runners should ensure that they have vivid and controlled images when visualizing an upcoming training run or race. Vivid images include both the emotional and environmental detail of the event. Using all your senses will help create both clear and detailed images of how you will feel (emotions) and what you will see (environment). Controlled images should center on factors you can control. For example, do not visualize the weather miraculously changing from rain to sun since you have no control over the weather. However, seeing yourself pick up the pace and work through adversity is completely within your control. Only you have control over how you think about your performance. If you want to see success, choose to visualize success.

Controlling your images and including vivid details are keys to successful imagery training

A runner may visualize themselves from one of two perspectives; internal or external. Internal imagery is viewing oneself from a first-person perspective. A runner would therefore be visualizing from their own vantage point, seeing what they would see if actually running. This method lets the runner feel the execution of their movements. External imagery, on the other hand, is viewing oneself from a third-person perspective. In this scenario, a runner will take in the whole environment and watch their successful performance from afar. What do you look like as you run up the hill? How is your form? Do you look fatigued? Is your foot striking the ground in proper alignment with the rest of your body? There is no right or wrong way to visualize. Many runners will use a combination of internal and external imagery so they can both *feel* the movement and *see* their performance.

Visualizing the environment, having vivid and controlled images, taking both a first- and third-person perspective, and maintaining positive images are the keys to effective imagery. Above all, have realistic expectations of what imagery can do for you. Imagery training alone will not turn you into a qualified marathoner if you are struggling to cross the finish line in under six hours. Imagery can help maximize your potential and help you attain your highest level of performance.

> *Internal imagery allows a runner to 'experience' a run*
>
> *External imagery allows a runner to 'see' the run*

Imagery Triggers & Scripts

Once you become comfortable with the visualization process, you can take your imagery training one step further by developing imagery triggers and imagery scripts. Imagery triggers are certain words, phrases or images you associate with a past successful performance. One runner I worked with had told me about a peak performance he had during a half-marathon. He underwent an intense training program to help him achieve a personal best and was rewarded with his fastest finishing time for a half-marathon. As he described the performance, a few aspects stuck out. First was his mantra – "The conditions are tough, but I'm tougher than the conditions," which resulted from the dreadful wind, cold rain and challenging course. Second was his attire. He wore a red Addidas tank top and blue Umbro soccer shorts. Why is this relevant? Because every time he is struggling on a run, he repeats his mantra and recalls the image of himself in that attire, triggering the feelings of triumph and achievement to get him over his struggles.

Writing imagery scripts allows runners to create their own reality of how they foresee their upcoming events unfolding. Essentially, think about one of your best runs and imagine doing that in your upcoming training run or marathon. The script should be read numerous times so you can learn to connect with the thoughts, feelings and emotions you have identified. You should also have the script read to you a number of times so you can relax and allow the performance to happen in your mind.

The imagery script found on page 55 was created for runners training for the Boston Marathon. The 20-mile run is typically the longest run when training for a marathon and can be quite a stress-inducing event. The run itself is fine; it's more the anticipation of the run that can cause apprehension. For the runners, the act of reading through this script allowed them to become more familiar with sections of the course with which they were unfamiliar. The purpose of the script is to make the runners feel as if they have already run the 20-miler. They would feel more comfortable in the environment, they would recognize sights and landmarks, they would be in tune with their body and mind, and they would know how they should feel and how they should think during certain stretches of the run. When creating your own imagery script, make sure you do the following:

- Begin with your arrival at the start of race
- Include your normal routine and preparation
- See and feel yourself stretching well during your warm-up
- Use vivid detail by including sounds, smells, colors, etc
- Use energizing, positive, and confidence-building words
- Include controlled images of how you would like to run

After the 20-mile run, many of the runners asked me if I had a script prepared for the final 6.2 miles. I did not. But I explained to them that they should take advantage of the fact that they all live in Boston and should either run the final 6.2 miles one day or drive the course to see what they are in store for. After experiencing the final stretch for themselves, they could then script out their own reality for the finish.

Do not be troubled by the length of the following script. Scripts do not necessarily have to be this long, but covering 20 miles of the marathon course can get rather extensive. Runners may also create a script for shorter runs which will reduce the length. The grammar in this script is far from perfect, but that was done on purpose. A marathoner is not likely to speak in full sentences with spot-on grammar when running 26.2 miles. This script will raise your sense of self-awareness and help you experience what it will be like to run the first 20 miles of the Boston Marathon.

Imagery Script for 20-Mile Run

BEEP BEEP BEEP. What the? Ugh, my alarm! Up and out of bed. Today is the day, the big 20-miler – feel the energy, feel the excitement, embrace the challenge. Looks nice outside, sun is starting to shine, hopefully it won't be too cold. Feeling a little nervous for this one. Just want to stick to my routine, eat my normal breakfast, put on my running gear and head out to Wellesley and jump on the bus to Hopkinton.

I arrive at the Wellesley Community Center, get out of my car, feel the cool spring morning breeze on my face, and see my fellow runners. I drop my bags in the meeting room, greet the familiar faces and head for the bus. First mental check of the day – what am I thinking about? Need to focus on myself right now, make sure I have eaten enough, hydrated well, and stretched properly. Check, Check, Check. No thoughts on factors outside my control like the weather, how long it will take us to get out there, what other runners did this morning, etc. Right now, it's all about what I need to do to ensure a positive and successful training run. Uh oh, I have those butterflies. Is this normal? I feel sick; am I going to throw up? What's wrong with me? Wait a minute, stop those thoughts, it's just me overreacting again and making this 20-miler larger than life. Hey, I just ran 18 miles last weekend so I know I can do this. Positive thoughts, positive feelings, positive performance. This is going to be an outstanding day. A dress rehearsal for the real thing. Water stops are planted along the way, I have my sport beans and other food I may need. I'm prepared, confident and ready to go. I'm ready to socialize with the other runners on the bus and psych up (or down) for the run.

As we arrive in Hopkinton, I notice that this is nothing like what I expected. But then again, I have never been here so why am I surprised? Stop worrying about something that is not relevant and is out of my control. Back to present moment. This is important – keep my thoughts on the present as often as possible because it's the only thing I have control over. I follow the runners off the bus and see the big gazebo near the start. I take a moment to visualize what it's going to be like on marathon day with 20,000 other runners milling around. What a sight it will be. This gets me excited and energized. Remember, start out slow, nice easy pace, and let the run just happen. Do not force anything, RUN MY RUN. One last trip to the restroom (or woods) and I'm ready to start. The less I procrastinate, the sooner I finish. Nerves are racing through my body but they are good nerves. This shows I am ready, prepared and excited for the upcoming challenge. I'm an athlete, I'm a runner, I persevere and never give up. I stroll to the starting line, appreciate the moment, start my watch, and embark on the latest journey of my marathon training.

The first mile starts out with an immediate descent out of Hopkinton. Keep it slow, keep it steady, save the quads for later. The course takes me up a slight little incline and into some rolling hills. Nothing new to me, just getting used to the course. I feel a few aches and pains – but with 19 more miles to go I make it a point to not blow this out of proportion. The first few miles of any long run tend to be a struggle, just need to work out the kinks. The weather is cool but pleasant – much better than the arctic freeze I have been accustomed to this winter. As I approach the 1-mile marker, I see a nursery on the left. Mile 2 starts out pretty flat then leads into a small decline as I enter Ashland. Using some self-talk, I stress the importance of not running these downhills too fast. Remember, slow and steady, find my groove and stay focused on the present. Within the second mile, I notice a bar up on the left and the marathon market deli on my right. Mile 2 comes and goes and I'm still working out the kinks. Mile 3 also starts out fairly flat and eventually leads into a slight incline and soon I see Ashland State Park on the right. I take a few moments to look at everything that is surrounding me. The more familiar I become with the course, the more comfortable I'll be on marathon day. Running at a nice, easy, smooth pace, I pass the mile 3 marker and see Ashland High School on my left and Dunkin Donuts. Time for a quick body scan. How am I feeling? If it's time to have some water, make sure I drink it now and stay well hydrated. Energy is feeling fine. My diet the past few days has been solid so I feel like I am properly fueled. As mile 4 begins, I see Brooks Pharmacy on the left and CVS on the right. The course is somewhat up and down right now. Not quite what I had expected, but then again, I am completely unfamiliar with this course. Feeling good right now. Look at all of these other runners out here. What a great day. Couldn't ask for better weather. Take in some deep breaths and feel myself get stronger every time I inhale. Breathe in that cool, clean air. The road flattens out a bit as I approach the end of mile 4 and I see Dairy Queen on the right and Fitzy's Car Wash.

Mile 5 is starting out nice and flat; just what I needed. Finally feeling comfortable with the run. Legs feel strong, body feels good and my mind is focused. Continuing down Route 135, the road begins to wind. It's nice to take some time and talk to the other runners surrounding me and see how they are doing. I still try to picture what things will be like on marathon day with so many spectators. This gets me pretty jazzed and I feel my pace picking up. Trigger Word – slow down, stay at your pace, and focus back on the here-and-now. As mile 5 comes to an end, the course starts to descend into the town of Framingham and I go through my mental checklist (make sure my thoughts are positive and focused on the present). As I trek into mile 6, the course turns uphill and then flattens out. As I pass by some gas stations and car dealerships, I come across the Framingham train station (would love to jump on that right now and just finish). Stop that thought and focus on the run. After the train station I see the Chicken Bone Saloon on the right – ever wonder what goes on in that place? Okay, feeling strong as I push on into mile 7. The road flattens out again and this gives me a chance to catch my breath, focus on my breathing and pop a few sport beans for a little energy. Just past the 7.5 mile mark, I enter Natick and run up another hill. Wow, this course is a lot hillier than I thought, so glad I am running it now. I see the West Natick train station as I plow into mile 8. It's getting hard not to think about the remaining 12 miles I still have, but it's paramount that I keep my focus on getting through the next mile. Those sport beans have given me that boost of energy I needed. Feeling good, feeling strong, legs still feel fresh, chest is wide open, breathing is easy, confidence is high, and I feel zoned-in right now. Mile 9 starts out relatively flat but then morphs into more rolling hills. Take it slow, run it smart. My stride feels easy and smooth. No pain, no discomfort, everything is clicking. Mile 9 is winding down and I see the Natick animal clinic on my left, a frozen lake/pond on my right and those train tracks on my left. Approaching the halfway point of this run, mile 10 starts out relatively flat and then transforms into some peaks and valleys. Now I'm feeling like a human roller coaster going up and down these rolling hills but I am handling them well and have great self-awareness. The 10th mile is coming to a close as I approach Natick Center.

Mile 11 serves up a flat road but then a hill quickly emerges. Strong and powerful strides up the hill. Use my glutes and keep the hamstrings strong. Big deep breaths as I power up the hill. Feel strong, feel good. Drink some more water and prepare myself for the back half of this run. Mile 11 comes and goes and I charge right into mile 12. Time to kick it into another gear. My mind seems totally focused on this run. It's like I am in that runner's zone – that state of total control…a state of flow – everything is feeling easy and efficient. Running downhill for a bit allows me to catch my breath. Road turns uphill – strong, powerful strides up this hill. Mile 12 greets me with a steep descent into Wellesley. I see the sports fields on the right and run past Wellesley College. This is going to be fun on marathon day. All those girls screaming and cheering and their energy just pushing you through that stretch. Okay, refocus back on the run. Let's take a moment to notice all the other runners and everything else that is happening around me. The sound of the other runners, my own breathing, and the soft contact my foot makes with the pavement. What a great day to be out here. I'm approaching the halfway point of the marathon, mile 13, and I feel strong.

After passing Wellesley College, there is a small downhill that leads into a little shopping center. This is starting to look familiar to me. Oh yes, I just ran this section of the course the past few weeks. I know exactly where I am. This is the familiar part of the course and it makes me feel more confident, comfortable, and at ease with the run. Heading into mile 14, I see the Wellesley library on the right as well as the break off to Route 16. Road is pretty flat and a slight descent is not too far away. As I make my way past the mile 14 marker, I can see a field on my right and I know I'm only moments away from my Saturday morning home, the Wellesley Community Center. I pass through the sign for Babson College and continue down Route 16 and see Marathon Sports on my left and Brigham's Ice Cream on my right. Need to refocus my thoughts back to the run. How am I feeling right now? Anything hurting? How is my energy? Do I need to pop any more sport beans? Feeling good, feeling strong, and feeling like I'm hitting my groove. I pass by the Wellesley Community Center and cruise past the mile 15 marker. Five more miles to go – home stretch.

Entering mile 16, the course is beginning to descend so take it slow on the downhill to save my quads; the Comm Ave hills will be here soon. Easy strides, easy breaths – I am running at a great pace with balance, poise and control. About halfway through mile 16, I see Papa Razzi on my right and on my left is that Grossman's Hardware store. Mental and physical check time – how am

I feeling? Do I need to slow it down? Can I maintain this pace? Need to listen to my body as I'm in the last segment of the run with plenty of hills still to come. I now find myself entering Newton Lower Falls as I begin mile 17. Here comes that sneaky hill up and over Route 128. Positive thoughts – I love this hill because it's preparing me for the three-headed monster that's creeping closer. I pass 128 and run through the intersection of Beacon and Washington. Enjoy the last slight downhill and straightaway for a while and conserve my energy. This is where I have a choice – become terrified or intimidated by the upcoming turn on to Comm Ave or start using some positive self-talk and affirmations to get me psyched for the hills. I amble past Newton-Wellesley Hospital and wrap up mile 17 after the Woodland T-Stop. One more time to scan my body for any unusual aches and pains (I have been running for 17 miles!), but everything seems to be fine. I pop a sport bean for some extra juice, feel the energy flow through my body, and set my sights on Route 30. This is where the race begins. The first 17.5 miles was just a warm-up, now comes the real running. I make the right turn on to Comm Ave and visualize what it will be like on Marathon Day with thousands of people yelling, screaming and cheering. Port-o-Johns will be on that island dividing the main road from the access road, music will be blaring, the fire station will be rocking, and it's going to be intense! Okay, need to focus again – back to the present time. Here it is, Hill #1. I've done this many times. One thing I do know is that I LOVE HILLS.

Putting a big smile on my face and reciting some motivating song lyrics, I power my way up the hill, always looking ahead. With each step I take, I'm getting closer to the top. Wow this feels great. With each breath I take in, I feel myself getting stronger. With each exhale I take, I'm eliminating any negativity, stress or pain. Another big breath in – power, strength, energy; another big exhale – out with the negativity. These hills have nothing on me, that's right – NOTHING! Big deep breath when I get to the top, one hill down, two to go, and I have just passed the 18 mile mark. Time to scan the body again, make sure everything is still working (which it is), but feel slight tenderness in my calf and hamstring. No big deal, I'll stretch out for a few seconds. Nothing wrong with stretching, need to do whatever I have to do to finish. Stop, stretch, and continue. Feel much better. What a great day. I can feel the warmth of the sun on my skin, see the sights of the route and hear the sounds of the multitude of runners. This is why I have trained for the past three months in sub-zero temps and copious amounts of snow and slush – for days like today. FOCUS! Need to get my mind back on the run – back in the present, back in the zone – it's the only thing I can control. The second hill is on its way so focus on what I need to do to cover this stretch and then I'll make my game plan for the final push. Continue to breathe in that crisp spring air. Feel the adrenaline rush from the last sport bean. Mile 19 finds me with a brief straightaway – great recovery for my legs, which are definitely feeling heavy right now. It's okay though, I run with ease and comfort, this is my day! Mile 19 comes to an end as I pass through Homer St and prepare for Hill #2.

Here it is, mile 20. How in the world did I make it to this point? No time to think about the past. Focus on the upcoming challenge. Make sure to replace any grimaces and tension with a smile and remind myself that I love the challenge this course is providing me right now. All told, I feel pretty damn good. Sure I am a little sore in my hamstrings and calves (and craving a peanut butter and jelly sandwich), but that is irrelevant now. I had the right mix of sport beans, water and Gatorade. Confidence is at an all-time high. As I run up what seems to be an endless incline my focus is on the tightness of my calves and hamstrings. When is this hill ever going to end? This seems like an eternity. This thing is a killer. Holy s**t this thing is tough. Am I going to be able to run 6 more miles the day of the marathon? STOP! Stop those negative thoughts. How can these thoughts possibly help my performance right now? For the past 30 seconds I have done nothing but put myself down. I start thinking of the reasons why I am running this marathon, the person I am running for. I begin picturing the people who have supported me and that funny story somebody told me earlier. That ear-to-ear smile slowly reemerges on my face and I feel loose, relaxed, calm, confident and focused. Just imagine that there is a magnet at the top of the hill, pulling me closer and closer. My stride feels smooth, easy and effortless. There it is, the top of Hill #2. Big deep breath, I feel strong, powerful, energized, focused and determined. The course flattens out again. I see a large contingent of TNT runners as I eventually come up on the Centre St intersection – the magical 20-mile marker.

I now have the most important asset heading into the marathon – a positive, successful experience of running the course. Sure I'm tired, but on race day, I'll have 20,000 other runners, and hundreds of thousands of spectators cheering me on for the final 6.2 miles. I bring myself to a slow walk and stretch out the legs and calves. Ah that feels great. Wow, what a day. Three to four months ago, the thought of a 20-mile run seemed like an implausible fantasy, now it's my reality. I can do this, I will do this. Come April 21st – I WILL BE AT MY PEAK!

When beginning your imagery training, it is best to seek out a quiet setting to minimize distractions. This can help you develop a level of relaxed concentration so you can focus solely on the thoughts and images for your upcoming run. Many runners will begin with a few daily imagery sessions (lasting 3-5 minutes) as they learn to master this mental skill. Integrating mental imagery into your daily training is actually quite simple. For instance, as you shut off your television and get ready for bed, allow yourself some time to visualize specific aspects of the next day's run. When you awake in the morning, take an extra few minutes in bed to anticipate the upcoming run. If you are planning to run after work, take a few minutes during the day to visualize your route. If you have trouble seeing detailed images or have difficulty controlling your image, do not give up. The more you practice imagery, the easier it will become to control what goes on in your mind. Successfully managing what happens between the ears and staying focused on the present moment is a challenge every runner embraces.

MENTALLY TOUGH RUNNING: STRATEGY #10

🏃 **Identify potential imagery triggers that you can think about during times of struggle:**

🏃 **Create your own imagery script for an upcoming run and eventually one for the marathon. Remember to include clear and controlled images and incorporate all the five senses to make your imagery feel as real as possible:**

CHAPTER 6: RUNNING IN THE MOMENT

"Trouble ahead, trouble behind, and you know that notion just crossed my mind"

The day of the 2002 Boston Marathon had finally arrived. Along with a few other friends, Bubbles and I hopped in the car and headed toward Hopkinton. The days, weeks and months of training were over. It was now time to perform. We had no idea what to expect in the coming hours but we were certainly eager to find out. Like many first-time runners, our thoughts were all over the map. With this unbalanced pattern of thinking, we were starting to make each other crazy. But I quickly remembered Jay's last words of wisdom – "For possibly the only time in your life, you will feel like a professional athlete. Spectators will be screaming your name and kids will want to give you a high five. Enjoy the day and keep your eye on the prize." It sounds so simple; just focus on what is happening *now* and let the marathon happen.

Bubbles and I started out running together. One of the visual benefits of starting at the back of the pack of the Boston Marathon is that the course immediately descends and you have an incredible view of 20,000 runners starting their own personal journey. Recalling what Jay had told us, we just soaked in the moment for the first few miles and enjoyed the sights and sounds of the marathon. The first sign that something was amiss occurred around mile 4. Bubbles had looked at his watch and noticed that it had already been about an hour since the race had started. One of the drawbacks of starting at the back of the pack is that it had taken us about 15-20 minutes to actually cross the starting line. What made this such a problem? Bubbles' wife had flown in from Chicago for the race and was waiting to see him at mile 24. She had a flight scheduled for 5:30 p.m. out of Boston because she needed to get back home for work. The race started at noon and Bubbles figured it would take him about four hours to get to mile 24. This would have given his wife plenty of time to see him and then jump in a cab and head to the airport. What Bubbles did not anticipate was the additional 20 minutes it would take just to get to the starting line. So after doing some quick math, he turned to me and said, "I need to run the next 20 miles in just over three hours in order to see my wife before she has to leave." Panic and disappointment painted his face. He was realistic about his abilities as a runner and knew it was going to be a matter of minutes – provided everything went well. We continued on our way and felt great physically. Mentally, it was a different story for Bubbles as he played out all the scenarios:

- ♦ "If I had known it was going to take 20 minutes to cross the starting line, I would have had her take a later flight."
- ♦ "I should've had her wait for me at mile 13 as it would've still given her plenty of time to get to the airport."
- ♦ "I'll be so bummed if I don't get to see her."
- ♦ "Maybe she'll skip her flight and just to wait for me."

The problem with the 'what if' scenarios was that his mind was vacillating between the past and the future. There was no stopping in the present moment, and this actually began to take a toll on him physically. Just past mile 14 we saw my college roommate, so we stopped to say "hi" for a minute. At this point, Bubbles sat down to stretch, put his head back, and muttered – "I feel spent. I need to take a nap." Of course he was kidding (sort of), but I made it a point to get him back up and running. I told him to remain focused on the moment. He was 10 miles away from seeing his wife and it would all work out. Just take it one mile at a time. We pushed on. Bubbles was staggering down Beacon Street, approaching mile 24 when he saw a cab pulling over and someone about to get in. It was, of course, his wife. At the last moment, she turned around to check for him one more time…and there he was. It had all worked out. He saw his wife and finished the race. A simple twist of fate.

It has been over seven years since that day in Boston and Bubbles still talks about how he was never able to truly enjoy and appreciate running the Boston Marathon – his only marathon.

This was a classic case of how the mind of a runner can wander far into an uneasy future or stray deep into a problematic past. Focusing on these troubles will not only affect your mind, but it may also have debilitating consequences on your body. Experiencing race anxiety and having your thoughts wander are typical. But a runner will only think and feel like this if they choose to think and feel this way. A runner may endure 15 miles of uncontrollable, inconsequential and meaningless thoughts if they *choose* to have uncontrollable, inconsequential and meaningless thoughts. The proverbial 'running zone' calls for a runner to stay locked in the present moment to center both the body and the mind.

The following concepts, strategies and techniques are essential in helping a runner focus on the moment, forget about the past, and leave their worries behind.

Controlling the Controllables

The 2005 Boston Marathon presented runners with an extremely demanding challenge – beat the heat. The majority of runners training for the race had faced a familiar New England winter. They were accustomed to temperatures 40 degrees or below, not the spike in weather conditions they were about to experience. The day before the race, the temperature was in the mid to high 40s, which was normal for that time of year in Boston. Race day brought the runners a treat they would not soon forget...a 40 degree *rise* in temperature. With the neurotic personalities of marathon runners, I am quite confident that the Weather Channel website server almost crashed with the number of people checking to see just how brutal Marathon Monday was going to be. The 87 degree day was the second highest on record for the marathon. On the bus ride from Boston to Hopkinton that morning, many runners were discussing the scorching weather forecast and their impending doom. Here is a sampling of what I heard on the ride:

- Did you hear how hot it is supposed to be today?

- I heard it could get into the 80s before the race even begins.

- I heard that it might get into the 90s today.

- I can't believe all my training will be wasted.

- How is this possible?

- It's just not fair!

- If it had been warm all week, then maybe we would have had a chance to acclimate

- What am I going to do? I'm going to die out there!

After 10-15 minutes of listening to these discussions, I asked one of the runners why they were focusing so much on the weather. His answer was quite simple – "Because it's going to be 90 degrees today, that's why." I said to him, "I know it's going to be 90 degrees today, but for the last 15 minutes you've all been talking about how bad it's going to be. You can't do anything about the weather, you do not control the weather, and you cannot change the weather, so why worry about the weather? You need to think about yourself and what you can do to successfully handle the weather." I went on to tell him that the more you think about the weather and all the potential negative consequences, the more stress you'll have. With four hours to go before the marathon, a runner needs additional stress as much as we need another reality television show. He agreed and we spent the next 20 minutes discussing strategies on how to actually deal with the problem, making him feel much more relaxed and prepared for what was to come during the marathon.

It is quite common for runners to focus on factors outside of their control, especially during challenging and trying times. I make it a point to ask my runners how they are feeling and what they are thinking about before a long run. If I get the sense that the runner is worried or nervous, I'll ask them why. Typical responses include: "I was up late last night and didn't get much sleep," "I have so much work to do for my job," and "I had such terrible runs this week that I don't think today will be any better." The runner cannot change whether or not they went to sleep late the previous night, they cannot change the amount of work they have to do next week, and they cannot change how their runs went earlier in the week. They have no control over what is causing their apprehension. If you cannot change the cause of the anxiety then stop thinking about it and change your focus to something you can control.

> **Letting go of the uncontrollables associated with a run will reduce stress, worry, and anxiety**

The following factors are just a sample of aspects relating to running that you can and cannot control.

Controllables:

♦ Your effort, preparation, goals, nutritional habits, thoughts, rituals, the present moment, etc

Uncontrollables:

♦ The weather, start time of run/race, shoe string breaking, the course, etc

---

MENTALLY STRONG RUNNING: STRATEGY #11

✎ **Identify all the things you can control for your runs and the marathon:**

✎ **Identify all the things you cannot control for your runs and the marathon:**

Rituals and Routines

Runners are creatures of habit. They get accustomed to doing things a certain way and never like to break tradition. Whether it's eating certain foods the night before a run, wearing a particular shirt that has special meaning, listening to certain songs during a run, or always running at the same time every morning – runners develop tendencies that only make sense to them. These tendencies are also know as routines or rituals. They come in handy when planning for an upcoming training run and are extremely beneficial when preparing for the marathon. Routines allow runners to feel as if they have control over their performance and help them keep their focus in the present moment. Every runner has their own customs, idiosyncrasies, habits and quirks when preparing for a run. Your routine should be designed around your own distinctive personality and characteristics. You must do what feels right for you.

The purpose of a routine is to make *you* feel in control of your run. You should not allow the routine to control you. Then it becomes a superstition and possibly a negative self-fulfilling prophecy. The following story illustrates this point.

The night before a long run, Corey would check his GPS watch to make sure it was charged up, eat his dinner before 8:00, and lay out his clothes for the next day's run before he went to sleep. Upon wakening, he would stretch his calves, quads, and hamstrings; eat a bagel; and drink two glasses of water. Further, Corey always wore his favorite black shorts and socks on these long runs. There was something special about those socks. Every time he wore them for a long run, he ran exceptionally well. He wasn't sure why he ran so well in them, he just did. By following his routine, Corey felt prepared, focused, confident, and ready to run. This routine became habit and was followed week after week. Although it did not translate into successful runs all the time, Corey felt as if he was going to have success before every long run. That feeling of control was the key in building his confidence. One day on a 16-mile run, the routine began to control Corey. After finishing his breakfast and pre-run stretching, Corey began his run.

About two miles in, he realized that his GPS watch was not charged and it shut off. Corey was at a loss. What in the world was he going to do now that his trusty training companion had shut down? Instead of categorizing this problem as being 'out of his control,' Corey chose to become frustrated over this unfortunate turn of events. Mentally, Corey was unable to focus properly on the run. He continually thought about his estimated mileage and pace, and struggled mightily throughout the remaining 14 miles. He had learned his lesson to separate what was in his control and what was out his control, and to keep his mind on the process of running.

What benefits are gained from dwelling on the 'what ifs?' There was no way to know exactly how far and fast Corey had run so there was no reason to stay focused on this uncontrollable thought. This experience ultimately paid immeasurable dividends for his marathon. Corey packed up and traveled to New York for the NYC Marathon. While getting dressed the morning of the race he realized he had forgotten his favorite black socks. Instead of believing this unintentional miscue would lead to a poor performance, Corey managed to block it out by focusing on his goals, positive trigger words, and a smooth, controlled breathing pattern. Corey finished the race by setting a personal best and attributed his success to his mental preparation and race day mantra of "With every breath I take, I get stronger."

When establishing an effective routine or developing unique rituals for your training runs, use the following guidelines:

- Identify what you like to do the night before your long run.
  - What do you like to eat for dinner?
  - What time do you like to eat dinner?
  - Do you like to load your iPod?
  - Do you enjoy staying home and watching a movie?
  - What time would you like to go to bed?

- Identify what you like to do the morning of your long run.

  ♦ What time will you wake up?

  ♦ What will you eat and drink?

  ♦ What will you wear?

  ♦ What stretches do you like to do?

- Identify what you like to do during the run.

  ♦ Do you visualize the route moments before starting?

  ♦ Do you like a particular sports drink or energy booster?

When establishing a routine for the marathon, use the following guidelines:

- Do not stray far from what you have been doing during your training. Keep things as normal as possible. Whatever you like to eat the morning of a long run – eat it marathon morning. This is not the time to try something new and different. Consider the following story:

  ♦ Many runners will use a substance called Body Glide or Vaseline to help prevent chafing in different areas of the body. About 20 minutes before the start of a marathon, a runner noticed people smearing Vaseline on their feet. Curious, he asked them what they were doing. After receiving the explanation and an invitation to try it himself, he thought it would be a good idea. Bad move! As the race began and he started to run, he felt his feet slipping around in his sneakers. He couldn't tolerate this sensation and had to run off the course, take his shoes off and wipe the Vaseline off his feet with his shirt. This incident threw off his whole day. So I repeat, DO NOT TRY ANYTHING NEW ON MARATHON DAY!!!!

- Make a list of everything (and I mean *everything*) you need to do between now and the race. Do not leave things to the last minute.

  - Do you have all of your race day supplements (food, gear, music)?

  - Do you have your shirt and shorts picked out?

  - What do you plan on doing over the weekend?

  - What time would you like to go to sleep on marathon weekend?

  - What would you like to have for dinner the night before?

  - What time do you plan on waking up on race day?

  - What time are you catching the bus or driving to the start?

Consistent preparation leads to consistent performance

Like any new skill, a routine may seem awkward or uncomfortable at first. Use your training runs to make your routines *routine*. The more you prepare the more in control you will feel. Having a strong sense of personal control going into the marathon is a great way to increase confidence and keep your focus on the race.

MENTALLY TOUGH RUNNING: STRATEGY #12

Develop your own rituals and routines using the guidelines specified above. Remember to think of everything you would like to do the night before a run, the morning of a run, pre-run, during the run, and post-run:

A Change of Mind

In 2006 the average time to finish a marathon was about 4 hours 40 minutes. That is a long time to be running, and the mind of a runner will wander thousands of times over the course of those 26.2 miles. It is nearly impossible to keep your mind completely focused on the act of running with so much time to ponder life and so many other things during your run. A runner needs to have the ability to focus on important or relevant information and maintain that focus for an appropriate amount of time.

Many runners have mentioned their inability to stay focused during their long runs. They claim to 'lose' their focus, which in turn, causes their running to suffer. They have sought my advice on how to improve on this 'apparent' problem. Before I do anything with them, I let them in on a critical little secret – they never truly lose their focus, they simply change their focus.

Let's think about this. The thought of losing something has a negative connotation. We rarely like to lose anything. Compound this issue by the fact that when we lose something, it is usually hard to find it or get it back. So, if you believe that you have lost your focus, you may believe you may never get it back. The reality is that the focus was never lost, it was simply changed. A runner has shifted their thoughts from one idea to the next. The suggestion of *changing* has more of a positive implication. After all, the only thing constant in the world is change, right? If you have the ability to change your thought once, you certainly have the ability to change your thought again – provided that you *choose* to change your thought back to what is most relevant at that particular moment. To better illustrate this concept, put yourself in the shoes of this runner and practice the following exercise:

When working with a runner with focus issues, the first thing I have them do is sit down for two minutes and just think about their upcoming run for the day. After two minutes I'll ask them what their final thought was. The vast majority mention that their last thought had nothing to do with running. It was just some random thought that popped into their head. So I put their focus problem into perspective. They cannot even stay focused on one thing for TWO minutes, how in the world can they expect to stay focused on one thing for over four hours? They see my point and feel better now that we were able to eradicate their focus problem.

Runners never lose their focus, they simply change it

Changing the Channel

If you notice that you are easily distracted by a random thought that *changes* your focus, try this very simple technique called 'Change the Channel.' Here is how it works. Imagine you're watching television and are extremely focused on the show that is on. Your level of alertness is probably very high. If someone comes into the room and takes the remote control and changes the channel to something you find extremely boring, your focus has most likely changed. Once that person leaves the room, what would you do? You would change the channel back to the show you were watching, thereby changing your focus. During your runs, try to change the channel when you notice you are thinking about and/or picturing something irrelevant or potentially harmful to your run. But make sure the 'channel' you change back to is displaying germane and pertinent thoughts that will get your mind back in the moment.

MENTALLY TOUGH RUNNING: STRATEGY #13

🏃 **Identify a few optimistic and relevant trigger words to focus on when your thoughts start to shift and betray you:**

But the question still remains: What should a runner actually think about to help them successfully finish a training run and, eventually, the marathon?

To Think or Not To Think – That is the question...

There comes a time during the marathon when an immovable force meets and irresistible object. It is that inevitable moment that many runners hope to never encounter, but, unfortunately, so often do. If you have run a marathon, you certainly know what I am talking about. It is simply known as 'the wall.' Hitting the wall is quite the agonizing and painful experience that can ruin months of training. Runners will experience physically unpleasant sensations such as a lack of coordination, nausea, muscle spasms, dehydration, and dizziness; as well as mental breakdowns such as an inability to think clearly and process what is happening around them. This uncomfortable quandary lends itself to increased frustration and drastically slower finishing times. While proper endurance training is certainly essential to avoiding such problems, proper cognitive training is just as important. Knowing what to think about can aid you in managing the cognitive peaks and valleys of 26.2 miles.

So how do you categorize the types of thoughts you have and determine which types of thoughts will help you succeed? The answer is relatively uncomplicated. Runners basically engage in associative and dissociative thinking strategies throughout their training runs and eventually the marathon. While each style has its benefits, knowing when to use the right approach will be indispensable come marathon day.

Associative thinking strategies are a great way to stay in the moment, as they require an attentional comittment to your body and a strict monitoring of any changes. Associative thoughts can be both internal and external. Such factors as your breathing rate, muscular fatigue, soreness, and thirst or hunger are internal factors that provide cues allowing you to properly pace, hydrate and nourish yourself. Being aware of your muscular sensations can help mask or minimize negligible pain or discomfort like blisters or chafing. While certainly uncomfortable, runners are not jeapordizing their overall health.

Thinking about your breathing will help keep your thoughts in the present moment since you are breathing in the present moment. If you want to keep your mind on what is *happening right now*, think about what you are *doing right now* – breathing (more on this in Chapter 7). By internally associating with your body, you can better gauge how your muscles feel. Are they warm, loose and energized? Or tight, stiff and cramped? Can you pick up the pace a little or do you need to slow it down? Associating internally every few miles can have tremendous benefits miles down the road. External association shifts the focus from your body to any number of task-relevent factors critical to success. Components such as race strategy, goals, mile markers, water stops and split times are all important aspects that will help in your overall performance.

Dissociative thinking strategies, which can also be internal and external, provide you with an opportunity to direct your focus on things that are task-irrelevant or *outside* your body. This is actually a form of advantageous distraction. When you can distract your mind from physical discomfort, it has the ability to enhance your run. But be mindful about any injuries. If you are tired or a little achy, that is one thing. Having a sharp pain in your knee, however, could signify a serious injury that needs attention. Some runners like to internally dissociate during segments of their run. In this case, a runner is thinking about something that will put them in a good mood. For example, some runners will sing a song to themselves while others may fantasize about winning the lottery. They temporarily go off into dreamland and think about how they would spend the money, whether or not they would quit their job, or where they might move to. The purpose of internally dissociating is to excite you and put you in a better frame of mind. Even though you are thinking about something that may never happen and something that has nothing to do with the run, you are proactively putting yourself in a positive, upbeat and energizing mood.

Some runners will take more of an organizational approach to their internal dissociation. They often think about what they need to do later that day or the work they have to do for the upcoming week. Runners do not stress about these tasks, they structure everything in their mind and plan their day or week out to make things seem quite manageable.

External dissociation occurs when you focus on something totally unrelated to the run. For example, rather than stressing about how many miles you have left to run, you may start counting how many red cars pass you by, how many blonde haired runners are on the street, or what the spectators are doing. In this case, you are purposely trying to get your mind off the physical and mental factors that are bothering you by enjoying the outdoor scenery and the competitive environment.

Associative and dissociative thinking strategies should be utilized in combination rather than isolation during long runs and the marathon. With the incalculable amount of thoughts circling through their minds runners will constantly switch from associating to dissociating. To best avoid a head-on collision with the 'wall' around mile 20, try to avoid internal dissociation as this type of thinking can hinder your awareness of important physical factors like running pace. Prolonged inattentiveness may cause you to start out too fast and subsequently bonk far before the race is over. Internally associating can help you monitor things such as pace, but too much of a cognitive emphasis on internal association may cause you to magnify or exaggerate physical discomfort. This too can cause you to hit the wall sooner and for a longer duration.

Ideally, you should use an amalgamation of external association and external dissociation. This way, you can minimize the effects of physical discomfort, enjoy the competitive environment, and keep your attention on the race-relevant tasks that are essential for achieving peak performance during the latter stages of a high-mileage training run and the marathon.

MENTALLY TOUGH RUNNING: STRATEGY #14

Identify a number of external associative and dissociative thoughts to help you cope with the latter stages of high-mileage training runs and the marathon:

As your mileage starts to increase dramatically, the pressure for success on these runs increases dramatically, too. Struggling through a long run will affect your confidence and focus. It is critical during times like this to stay in the moment as a runner's sense of control is truly tested. If you believe that an external factor will dictate your performance, you have given up your personal control and become more susceptible to failure. Making a commitment to exercise control during challenging situations can help you feel invincible, intense, properly focused and competitively relaxed. Keep your personal psychotherapy simple, as too much thinking leads to paralysis by analysis. Teach yourself to start thinking a lot about less and less.

CHAPTER 7: RELAXING ON THE RUN

"Been a hard day, nothing went too good, now we're gonna relax, everybody should"

If you carefully observe what runners do in the hour leading up to a race, you may be surprised to see many of them nowhere near the starting line. Most of them are in line for the Port-o-Johns. This could very well be the most popular area of the race. Why are so many runners congregated around the most foul and malodorous locale? Because they are uneasy, panicky and anxious for the race. But this is not necessarily a bad thing. Feeling nervous is a normal and natural sensation for anyone. If you don't have butterflies before a big run or the marathon, you better check your pulse to see if you are alive. After all, if you cannot get fired up for this ultimate personal challenge perhaps you should seek a new endeavor. The veracity of *experiencing* elevated levels of anxiety is one thing, but the manner in which a runner *interprets* the anxiety is a completely different story.

Training for a marathon can be stressful – but only if you choose to make it stressful. The day of the marathon can be ten times more stressful than the training – but only if you choose to believe it will be ten times more stressful. Are we sensing a common theme here? Our mind dictates the level of stress and pressure we will encounter. Some runners will respond well to the competitive challenges they face, whereas other runners will feel overwhelmed by the pressure and under perform.

Nerves are normal so treat them as a sign of excitement, thrill, and readiness to step up to the challenge

Why does this happen? From a psychological perspective, the mind begins to think it cannot succeed, creating thoughts of doubt. Physically, muscles begin to tighten up causing tension throughout the body. A mentally weak runner will interpret these feelings as an indication that they are not well-trained or that they are ill-prepared for the upcoming event. Conversely, mentally strong runners view any nervousness as positive energy. It is a sign that they are well-prepared for their run or race and are simply eager for the challenge. Let's now discuss how you can learn to overcome the common race-day worries.

Managing the Running Jitters

In Chapter 4, we learned how to overcome negative thoughts and maintain a positive mental attitude. Now we need to learn how to calm and relax the body. It may seem counterintuitive to relax your body before heading out for a run. After all, running is an active sport, so how could a relaxed body actually help us run better? Well, when your body is stressed your muscles become tense which makes even the easiest of movements feel difficult.

Understanding the concepts of arousal and anxiety, and how they can affect your body, is crucial to successfully handling the stressors that come with the territory. The term arousal is synonymous with intensity and excitement. It varies along a continuum from very low to very high. Think about your arousal or level of intensity right now. It's probably very low as you are sitting down and reading this book. Now think about your level of intensity or excitement as you watch the last minute of a basketball game with a tie score. There is a good chance your heart is racing, thus illustrating a high level of excitement. Your arousal or level of intensity is a positive quality that can help facilitate feelings of enthusiasm and competence during training runs and the marathon.

Feelings of anxiety are typically classified by worry, nervousness and pressure. Runners will experience anxiety in both their mind and in their body. Anxiety of the mind, known as cognitive anxiety, is characterized by thoughts of failure, self-doubt and negativity. Anxiety of the body, known as somatic anxiety, is exemplified with the butterflies, tense muscles and a racing heartbeat.

> *Arousal: positive mental state synonymous with intensity*
> *Anxiety: negative mental state marked by self- doubt*

Taking the concept of anxiety one step further, it is necessary to distinguish between the *state* anxiety and the *trait* anxiety of a runner. Your state anxiety is how anxious you feel right now or at a particular moment. State anxiety can change from one moment to the next.

You are minutes away from a meeting with your boss and you can feel your heart beating out of your chest. Your state anxiety is very high. Ten minutes later you are leaving your meeting with a 10% pay raise and suddenly your state anxiety is extremely low. Those thoughts and feelings of worry and dread have dissipated. An hour before you are heading out for your first 10-mile run you are likely to feel high state anxiety. You have never run this distance before and have thoughts of doubt. A mile into your run, a sense of calmness overtakes your body and the anxiety seems to melt away. State anxiety can be easy to manage, provided you have the proper mindset and strategies to deal with the moment-to-moment changes that are causing your uneasiness.

Trait anxiety is a little trickier. Your personality and how you generally feel or react to pressure situations will define your level of trait anxiety. This is a relatively stable factor than can influence your state anxiety in pressure situations, despite how well trained you are physically. The case of Bill will establish this concept.

Bill tends to be a very anxious and nervous person regardless of the task he is pursuing. This has led to low self-confidence. Bill has always enjoyed running and wanted to train for a marathon. He had run a number of 5-mile road races, and yet still felt just 'fairly confident' at running races of that distance. Bill would always doubt himself as race day approached but he would inevitably have a good run. This is simply his personality causing him to feel a certain way during important events. As he began training for his marathon he found himself feeling good about his ability to increase his mileage and quicken his pace. This increase in confidence actually led to a slight reduction in his state anxiety. Like many other runners, Bill suffered through a few forgettable runs. His propensity for becoming stressed under pressure threatened his goal of running the marathon. A runner with low state anxiety and high confidence has the ability to shake off a bad run and expect success on the next run. Yet after a few bad runs, Bill began convincing himself of his inability to succeed and would then experience high levels of state anxiety just prior to his long runs. Even though Bill had been successful on some previous long runs, he would focus on what could go wrong as opposed to what could go right. This began to take a toll on Bill psychologically as it heightened his state anxiety.

> *Interpret nerves as positive energy and a sign of being alive and use it to your benefit*

After consulting with me for a few weeks, Bill learned to accept his general anxiety and worked extremely hard to identify situations that caused him unnecessary stress. Because Bill was a highly-anxious person to begin with, there were two keys to regulating his anxiety:

1. De-emphasizing the outcome of the long runs
2. Simulation training

The long runs were a major source of stress for Bill. He would be very concerned with how long it took him to finish. If he ran 10 miles in 1:40 (a 10 minute pace) one week, he would put extra pressure on himself to keep that same pace the following week even though his mileage increased by two miles. This outcome orientation led to his anxiety. By de-emphasizing the importance of time on the long runs, and simply focusing on the process of finishing the distance, Bill developed the confidence to perform under pressure and appropriately deal with his running anxiety.

The second key was to have Bill undergo simulation training. Bill would prepare for each long run (regardless of whether or not it was 10 miles or 20 miles) as if it was the marathon itself. He would have to think about eating properly the night before the long run, wake up on time the next morning, give himself enough time to eat and stretch, etc. By training under these simulated pressure conditions, Bill became more familiar with the feelings of distress he would likely face on the day of the actual marathon. Any mistake or setback he encountered were viewed as building blocks and learning experiences which helped him gain the confidence and insight he needed to respond positively to his once incapacitating nerves.

Helping a runner cope with anxiety is a little more complex than it may seem. For best results, runners should clearly identify what type of anxiety they are suffering from. Is it more cognitive (negative thoughts), is it somatic (nervous feelings in the body), or is it a combination of both? If a runner is suffering from cognitive anxiety and they are being taught how to relax their body, the technique will prove to be impractical. Likewise, if the runner is burdened with the butterflies, it does not make sense to give him strategies to help monitor and change thoughts. If the runner is truly unaware of what causes the anxiety, it is best to give them a sampling of both thought and body relaxation techniques.

Warning Signs of High Anxiety

♦ *Clammy hands, negative self-talk, bewilderment*

♦ *Difficulty focusing, muscle tensions, dry mouth*

♦ *Butterflies, frequent trips to bathroom*

Some of strategies discussed in Chapter 4 may help you handle the negative thoughts that lead to cognitive anxiety. These strategies included: *Thought Reframing, Thought Stopping, and Positive Affirmations.* The following techniques are simple to learn and can help in reducing any tension and anxiety emanating from the body.

Deep Breathing

Perhaps the easiest relaxation technique to practice and learn is deep, or centered, breathing. It is a skill that you are actually quite efficient at performing. Are you breathing right now? If you answered "Yes," it not only means you are alive, but it also indicates that you are practicing the most basic technique to help relax, focus and calm your body. Deep breathing differs from normal breathing as the emphasis is on slow, controlled breathing from the stomach rather than the chest. Learning to monitor your breathing during a run can be extremely beneficial if you are feeling at all concerned or panicky. A runner will begin to feel anxious when they start worrying or stressing about a past or future event. Training yourself to direct your focus on your breathing when your mind curiously wanders is a great way to stay relaxed and in the moment. Controlling your breathing is symbolic of regrouping and recovering during stressful situations. The act of centered breathing can help you regain your composure and channel your energy and attention to the task at hand – the next mile. When practicing deep breathing, many runners find it helpful to generate positive images and thoughts in their mind with each inhalation and visualize any fatigue or negativity leaving their body with each exhalation. Using cue words and phrases such as 'energy in' or 'power' on the inhale, and 'out with the stress' on the exhale, can help produce energy and decrease any tension in your body. As discussed earlier, our friend Jay associated his breathing with strength – "With every breath I take, I get stronger." The simple act of breathing allowed him to feel stronger as the miles began to pile up.

Protocol for Deep Breathing:

- ♦ **Comfort** – find a quiet area where you can lie or sit down and loosen any restrictive clothing.

- ♦ **Concentration** – direct your focus on breathing from the stomach and let all other thoughts just come and go.

- ♦ **Control** – feel your body calm down and regain composure on every exhalation.

The effectiveness of this simple technique is evident from my own experiences. In January of 2004 I was asked to appear on a nationally-televised morning sports talk show. Having never been on television before, I was very excited for the opportunity to discuss my expertise. I felt like I was getting the red carpet treatment as the network had paid for my flight, arranged for a car service at the airport, and put me up at the hotel where they filmed the show. I was nervous yet confident about my upcoming segment and slept maybe three hours. I walked onto the set at 6:00 a.m. and was put into make-up. This is where the reality of the situation started to hit me. "Wow, I am going to be on national television in an hour." At 6:55 a.m. one of the production assistants came up to me and the other guest for the segment. She clipped on microphones and said that in three minutes we would be moved to the couch, the host would come over, and as soon as he began speaking we would be on the air. You can imagine what went through my mind. My heart started pounding, my breathing increased ten-fold and I began having a flurry of negative thoughts such as "What happens if nothing comes out of my mouth" and "What happens if I stutter over my words?" Then in an instant I was able to pull it together with some deep breathing. I told myself to take a moment, breathe slowly to regain my composure, and de-emphasize the 'importance' of the situation. Instead of thinking about the potential negatives, I put the situation into perspective.

"I am going to be sitting on a couch talking about sports. I do this every day of my life. The only difference is that I do not have cameras in my apartment. Keep my focus on the topics and I'll be okay." The simple act of deep breathing and thought restructuring helped to calm my nerves, build my confidence and refocus my thoughts.

Progressive Relaxation

This technique teaches runners to differentiate between a tense muscle and a relaxed muscle. This awareness is based on the concept that a muscle cannot be relaxed and tense at the same time. By contracting a muscle, a runner can identify tension in a specific area of the body. By relaxing the muscle, a runner can identify how to modify any existing tension for optimal performance during a run. This relaxation technique is a series of progressive scans of each muscle group. The process can be as long or as short as you like. With practice, it will become easier to identify certain muscle groups that seem to hold more tension than others. This may be useful just prior to a run if you feel some slight anxiety or tension. You can quickly recognize it, hold it, relax it, and then head out for a more peaceful and enjoyable run.

Protocol for Progressive Relaxation

♦ **Comfortable Position** – Lie on your back with your head, neck and trunk in line. Your legs should be straight and slightly apart with your heels pointing inward. Keep your arms down by your side, away from your thighs with palms facing up.

♦ **Breathe** – Inhale as you contract the muscle, exhale as you relax the muscle.

♦ **Contraction/Relaxation** – Contract each muscle for 5-10 seconds and then relax each muscle for 5-10 seconds.

♦ **Relax** – Starting with your head and ending with your feet, feel your entire body loosen and relax.

> *Do not force relaxation. Keep your mind focused, let it happen & enjoy the moment*

There are a number of additional methods and techniques that can help you relax your mind and body and decrease performance anxiety. These techniques include meditation, yoga, music therapy, imagery, and massage therapy. There is no single technique that will work better than another. Take the time to practice any of these techniques and go with what is most comfortable and effective for you.

Although long distance runners seem to have some common characteristics (like being crazy enough to want to run 26.2 miles), they are all wired differently. Some runners need to be 'psyched down' before a run while other runners may need to inject some energy into their body moments before they compete. Every runner needs to determine how he/she can alter their energy and intensity to maximize their training runs.

Energize Your Run

A technique you can practice to enhance awareness of your optimal level of intensity is the *Energy Dial*. Runners need to create a mental image of how intense they need to be to have a successful run. If you are going to engage in a speed workout at the track, you may need to crank up an 8 or a 9 on your dial. However, if you are about to embark on a 16-mile long run, you may want to tone down the intensity to a 4 or 5, as you'll need to conserve your energy throughout the run.

Knowing the proper level of intensity is a critical component to a successful run. Runners who are overly enthused for their long run are putting themselves at risk since they are likely to start out too fast and hit a wall. Although this high level of energy may look good on the outside, it will make for quite a laborious finish. Regulating intensity during training runs is a great way to prepare for the marathon. A common mistake by many marathoners is starting the race too fast. The adrenaline and excitement of the event can cause even the most experienced runner to come out too quick and subsequently ruin four months of training. Take advantage of the time you spend training to identify your ideal level of intensity for peak performance.

Activation Triggers

Similar to the energy dial where you are identifying the proper level of intensity you need for a particular training run, activation triggers can help you control your intensity during training and the marathon. Activation triggers can be a word, a phrase, or a simple movement like opening your hand or snapping your fingers. These triggers act like a light switch, turning on a feeling in your body that allows you to feel a certain way when you run. Runners will build an association between their mind and their body with their trigger. For example, the more a runner practices snapping his/her finger to increase their intensity, the quicker they will associate the act of snapping as a trigger to amplify their energy. With practice, and I stress the word *practice*, you will be able to say or think of your trigger and bring yourself to a proper level of activation for each and every run. The notion of self-suggestion purports that telling your body to act and feel a certain way can actually cause it to feel that way. The more you practice, the better your mind will be at telling your body how you want it to perform – in a relaxed, calm, controlled state.

Mentally strong runners accept the fact that they may feel nervous at times. They are able to differentiate between performance anxiety and performance excitement and channel their 'nervousness' into relaxed intensity. The desire to achieve and visualize success, the ability to stick to a plan, maintaining a positive mental attitude, keeping your thoughts in the moment, and staying calm under pressure are the mental ingredients needed to cook up a triumphant plate of miles. While these strategies can be independently beneficial, uniquely integrating all of them into training can help you achieve a state of ultimate awareness in which you are truly in control of your performance.

MENTALLY TOUGH RUNNING: STRATEGY #15

✎ Identify your warning signs of anxiety so you can handle
them more effectively during your runs:

✎ Develop a cognitive activation trigger to optimize your
competitive intensity:

✎ Using the Energy Dial, think about the level of intensity
you need to run your best. Give some reasons as to why
your level of intensity may need to fluctuate from time to
time:

CHAPTER 8: AWARE, ENGAGED AND IN THE ZONE

"Get in the groove and let the good times roll"

It's a cold, rainy December day as Jacob gears up for his daily run. He had just made the commitment to train for the 2009 Boston Marathon, and he knew he had to train under all types of conditions to be as primed as possible for the big day in April. After all, he did not want to pull a Charlie and be completely ill-prepared for a rainy marathon. The difference between the two runners was that Charlie purposely avoided such training conditions, whereas Jacob was embracing them. As Jacob was preparing for the run, he was picturing himself running in the rain, thinking about his route and taking pride in the fact that he would probably be the only person in his small New England town actually out for a run. Running in these conditions is certainly not easy as you need to be completely aware of your surroundings. For example, the roads may be slippery which can impact your running form; visibility may be challenging at times making it difficult to see what is in front of you; and cars will have an increased likelihood of skidding off the road which is clearly quite perilous to you. Conscious of these confounding factors, Jacob was able to lock in mentally for his run.

As he left his house to begin his 5-mile jaunt, the rain was soft and steady. It actually had the makings for a refreshing run. But a mile into his training, the rain began to come down much harder. At this point, Jacob questioned the situation and asked himself, "Do I turn around and go home or do I push on?" His decision was an easy one – push on. For starters he was already soaking wet so what was the point in turning around? Second, the time spent running in adverse weather conditions would only benefit him later on in training if faced with a similar dilemma. It was at that moment when everything seemed to click for Jacob. He was now fully engaged in the activity. What began as a potentially thorny run turned into an invigorating and cathartic experience for him. The last four miles of his run were arguably his best four miles in weeks. He felt in complete control of the run.

Reflecting on his training that day, Jacob indicated that time seemed to be passing slow and he felt in sync with every movement. There was absolutely no struggle for him on this day. It was as if the unfavorable environment strengthened him, both mentally and physically. Jacob was able to maintain such a positive mindset by:

♦ Clearly defining his goal for the day which gave him something specific to focus on during the run.

♦ Staying in the moment by listening to his Ipod.

♦ Keeping the weather conditions in perspective – "It's only rain, I'm not going to melt."

♦ Convincing himself that the run would make him mentally stronger for additional inclement runs.

♦ Taking pride that he was the only runner out on the streets.

Examining his reflections more closely, it is apparent that Jacob had integrated many of the concepts discussed in this book into this one daily training run. His thoughts were positive; he knew exactly what he wanted to do; he took some time to visualize himself running in these conditions; he took pride in his achievements; he was motivated to challenge himself and do something he knew others would not be doing; he focused on the moment and on factors he could control (his effort, the content of his thoughts, etc.); and he did not become overwhelmed by the uncontrollables (weather). All told, Jacob was in the zone.

For runners to achieve their full potential on marathon day, they need to cultivate a strong sense of self-awareness. Being totally aware of what is going on both inside your head and in your environment *at a particular moment* allows you to be in complete control of your running. A lack of awareness can lead to confusion, uncertainty, indecision and mental chaos; all of which are a recipe for disaster in the world of long-distance running. For a runner to develop self-awareness, they need to periodically 'check-in' on their current mental state. They need to assess their level of intensity, emotional state, thoughts and focus.

The best times to 'check-in' will vary from runner to runner. Some runners may need to check-in every mile, while others will self-evaluate every other mile or possibly every five miles. Remember, we are all wired differently so you need to experience your runs and keep a mental note of when you need to gauge your mental state of mind. As mentioned in Chapter 4, it is common for a runner to give into their pessimistic or frustrating thoughts. So instead of saying "I feel so horrible right now, I can't believe I have seven more miles to go," a runner needs to ask themselves a simple and straightforward constructive question like "How do I feel right now?" or "What am I actually thinking about right now?" These questions can provide answers concerning your level of intensity, emotions, thoughts, and what you are actually focusing on.

MENTALLY TOUGH RUNNING: STRATEGY #16

✎ **Answer the following questions during your training runs to help you identify when you should 'check-in' during the longer runs and the marathon to assure a successful run:**

1. How intense am I? Should I pick up the pace or slow down?

2. How am I feeling right now?

3. What am I thinking about right now?

4. What am I focused on right now?

Another benefit of having high self-awareness during a run is that it allows you to truly 'experience' each run rather than simply 'running another run.' What does it mean to truly experience a run? Think of your life right now. You are probably either working a job, in school, or maybe both. Think a little deeper into your situation. Are you simply *in a job* or are you *into your job*? Are you merely *in your classes* or are you *into your classes*? People who are only in a job or in a class are really just their physically. Their mind is elsewhere. When it comes to training for a marathon, you need to make a mental choice every time you go out for a run. Are you simply *in* another tedious run or are you *into* a stimulating and challenging run? By being aware, engaged and *into* your training, you will be better equipped to manage and control your thoughts, regulate your energy and intensity, and stay focused in the moment. This is the type of approach necessary to reach that magical state of mind where everything seems to come together.

> **You have a choice: be in a run…or BE INTO THE RUN**

The Running Zone

Have you ever experienced a run where everything felt effortless and smooth? A time when your mind and body were completely in sync? Perhaps you have experienced this state for the duration of a run or during particular moments of a run. During times like these, demanding tasks such as running a marathon seem to get easier. Runners are able to ignore pain and find a fluid rhythm as their mind and body merge into one. Whenever you have felt alive, focused, engaged, energized, in control, connected, composed, strong, confident, powerful, and in a groove, you have entered the most sought-after phenomenon every runner seeks – the zone. But do not confuse the concept of being in the zone with having an overall peak performance. A runner who has had a peak performance typically describes this experience as a time in which they performed at their highest level. Being in the zone is typically a transitory or temporary sensation. Although a runner will typically get into a zone when they are having a peak performance, it is not a precursor to a peak performance. You can have a horrible overall run but still manage to squeak out one or two miles where everything seemed to click. Getting into the zone is a plausible ambition for runners, but staying there for four hours is nearly impossible. The goal of every runner is to figure out a way to get into his/her zone as often as possible.

Being in the zone is also referred to as achieving a state of flow. It is a feeling or experience every distance runner strives to achieve and recapture. The $64,000 question is whether or not it is possible to train the mind to increase the probability of having a flow experience during training runs and the marathon. Many of the mental skills discussed up to this point can help you get into the zone, but there are also factors that can disrupt or prevent you from achieving this state of mind. Perhaps the most important element of being in the zone is to find the proper balance between the challenge you are facing and your skill level for that activity.

Entering the zone requires a runner to push themselves beyond their perceived limitations. But too far beyond (or too far below) may result in a quick departure from the zone. If your skill level is far greater than the challenge you face, a state of flow will not be reached because you are not being pushed to excel. If the challenge is too great for your skill level you may feel overwhelmed, thus causing flow not to happen. Having the appropriate balance between your skills and your upcoming challenge will help you reach the zone.

The marathon is a demanding challenge for anyone, including those who are highly trained. You may be thinking to yourself, "How in the world will my skill level ever match the level needed to complete the marathon? I've never even run a mile!" Finding your flow stems from your ability to turn any potential stressors into challenges; properly train to feel well prepared; have a clear focus on what you want to achieve; expend maximum effort; think confidently; and stay in the moment. You and I will never be elite runners. We are competitive recreational runners. So it is imperative that you trust yourself, trust your training, believe in the process, and let your performance just happen. This allows *you* to control your confidence rather than having the marathon influence your confidence. Just feeling that you can be successful in the marathon is of critical importance.

A great way to find the proper balance between the challenge of the marathon and your current skill level is to make a list of all the physical, mental, nutritional and general skills that will be critical to your overall success on training runs and marathon day. Some of these skills may be more significant than others, but they should all play a role in your upcoming run. Determine the significance of each skill and then rate your perceived ability for each skill. If you notice that a particular skill is extremely significant but you feel like you are severely lacking in that area, your ability to achieve a state of flow may be quite difficult. However, if your perceived ability for a skill is as high as the skill is significant, you have a great chance to reach the zone during a run. You are pushing yourself slightly beyond your capability which can help you get into the zone.

One runner identified the following skills as being essential to her overall success in training runs and the marathon. Level of significance for each skill and her perceived ability within that skill are displayed on a scale of 0-10 (10 being most significant).

	Significance	*Perceived Ability*
Physical:		
Flexibility	10	7.5
Mental:		
Positive Attitude	10	10
Nutritional:		
Hydration on Runs	9.5	7.0
General:		
Proper Shoes	10	10

As you can see from this table, our runner has identified some precise areas of her training where she needs to improve, as well as some areas where she feels really good. Flexibility is a significant physical skill for her overall success but she currently perceives herself at a level of 7.5. Properly hydrating on long runs is also seen as being a highly-significant nutritional skill; however she has realized that she still has some difficulty with finding the appropriate amount of fluid intake. If she were to do nothing about her flexibility and hydration issues, she would probably not experience a state of flow during her long runs or the marathon. She is likely to cramp up which can cause a myriad of problems. By being aware of her strengths and deficiencies, this runner has identified clear goals and has proactively taken steps to work on these specific issues.

MENTALLY TOUGH RUNNING: STRATEGY #17

Identify the essential skills needed for success and rate its significance and your perceived ability for each skill on a scale from 0 (not significant) to 10 (very significant):

	(0-10)	*(0-10)*
	Significance	*Perceived Ability*
Physical:		
Mental:		
Nutrition:		
General:		

Adapted, with permission, from S.A. Jackson & M. Csikszentmihalyi, 1999, Flow in Sport (Champaign, IL: Human Kinetics), 61.

So what are the essential mental components needed to get into the zone? What factors can prevent or disrupt our flow experience? The following three sections will answer these questions.

Zone Achievement

Achieving a state of flow begins, coincidentally, right where this book began; by having the motivation to achieve success. Runners with a high level of desire and competitiveness have superior feelings of competence. They may not be gifted physically and they may not be technically sound, but they have the mental strength and discipline to work as hard as they can every time they embark on a run. This mindset can significantly reduce performance anxiety as a runner is no longer worried about failing. Setbacks are viewed as building blocks simply because the runner has the resiliency to bounce back from challenging obstacles. Highly-motivated runners will have an optimal level of excitement before a run, feel relaxed yet energized, have the proper level of intensity for a given run, and truly enjoy their time out on the roads – all of which contribute to having a flow experience.

Believe it or not, you are the biggest barrier to having a flow experience. Forgetting about yourself and what others may think of you or expect from you leads to a loss of self-consciousness. Runners with no self-concern let themselves get lost in their run. They feel no outside pressures. They feel in control of their smooth, flowing and effortless movements. Time is transformed as hours will fly by like minutes, making a 15-mile run seem like a walk in the park. It is over before you know it. When a runner stops worrying about themselves they are free to become completely absorbed into their runs. An absence of self-consciousness will empower you, enhance positive self-perceptions, and fully engage you in your run.

Identifying specific physical and mental goals and achieving them in a timely manner are additional elements to achieving a state of flow.

Feeling physically prepared through proper training, rest, and good nutrition increases confidence. Going into a training run feeling in great shape physically gives you confidence that you can maintain a strong pace and complete the given mileage for the day. From a mental perspective, developing routines and rituals enables you to gain a sense of personal control over your performance, and helps you to feel better prepared for competition. A runner can facilitate flow on marathon day by having definitive race-day goals that help them handle the unexpected circumstances that occur during a run and keep their mind on the task at hand (the current mile they are running). Staying in the present and concentrating on the small details of a run will help you settle into a nice rhythm.

The environment can also play a role, as running in optimal climate conditions can heighten the chances of having a flow experience. There is nothing better than waking up marathon morning to temperatures in the high 40s or low 50s with a cool breeze and partly sunny skies. While a runner dreams of having perfect weather for the marathon, they are known to react rather excessively if the forecast calls for grim conditions. But even if the environment is less than desirable, how you choose to perceive the situation is actually more important. Conditions may be tough but you can be mentally tougher than the conditions. Remember, your level of self-confidence will serve as a major boost when trying to achieve a state of flow, even more so than your actual ability level. Believing you can be successful and having a positive mental attitude fosters self-assurance and helps runners get into and stay in the zone.

Zone Prevention

Perhaps the most destructive mental factor that can prevent a flow experience from occurring is having low motivation. Remember that motivation is a combination of where we direct our efforts and how much intensity we put into a particular activity. Failing to seek out personal challenges each week and putting less than 100% effort into your training can not only affect you mentally, it can also affect you physically. Minimal training intensity can cause a runner to feel unprepared physically for either a training run or the marathon. This in turn can lead to injuries, fatigue and feeling unfit. Trying to manage these harmful factors, which you could have prevented through disciplined training, can prevent you from achieving flow.

Even the elements that surround you can prevent you from entering the zone. A runner who is unable to deal with the demands of the marathon will find it extremely difficult to get into the proper mindset over the course of 26 miles. Feeling pressure from friends or even from one's own expectations will lead to a fragile mental state. The mind of a runner will be filled with negative thoughts and self-doubt. This will inevitably lead to low confidence, an inability to properly focus, a preoccupation with past and/or future events, and pre-competitive anxiety. Feeling too relaxed or having extremely high anxiety prior to a run or the marathon are additional factors that can prevent a runner from getting in the zone.

Zone Disruption

Once you get into a zone, the last thing you want is to disrupt this fluid mind-body experience. A lack of physical and mental readiness, negative situational influences, superfluous pressure, and an inappropriate focus all play a role in mentally interrupting your run. Not being physically ready to run due to poor conditioning will surely disrupt your flow when engrossed in a long 15-mile run. You may feel fantastic for the first few miles, but if you have not trained properly by gradually building your mileage, you are bound to hit the wall and break out of the zone. Constantly stopping during a run, incurring an injury, a shoelace becoming untied, or unsuccessfully coping with internal stress can lead to self-doubt, negative self-talk, and worrying too much about either the past, future or other uncontrollable events surrounding your run. All of which can put a screeching halt to an enchanted run.

If you take a closer look at the factors that can prevent or disrupt a flow experience, you will notice that you can control many of them. This further justifies the point that your success truly resides within your control. Moreover, being aware of these factors can help you recognize potential problems and identify proper coping strategies.

Getting in the zone does not happen by chance. The more you consciously try to get into the zone, the more elusive it will be. Flow is a controllable mental state of mind only in the sense that you can prepare yourself to experience this phenomenon through developing self-awareness and self-discipline.

Developing Awareness – Using a Running Journal

To develop self-awareness and a propensity for mentally getting into the zone for a run, you need to be conscious of what has helped your performance on training runs and what has impaired your performance. A valuable method for keeping track of successes and failures is the use of a running journal. This is a great way to evaluate your performance while giving you tremendous insight into both your advantageous and detrimental training habits. Consider the following case…

Todd was a relatively experienced runner, having run a number of half- and full marathons. Like many distance runners, Todd had his favorite pre-long run meal routines that he would rarely stray from. The only problem was that he would often battle stomach issues during his long runs and on the morning of his marathons. He simply attributed this to the normal anxiety a runner feels when preparing for a run of high mileage. Therefore, he kept to his routine of eating chicken and rice the night before his long runs while training for the Chicago Marathon in 2006.

Todd had made some major changes to this training regimen that year. He completely altered his workouts by following the *Run Less, Run Faster* running program that had served him wonderfully in his most recent half-marathon. Todd would partake in three specific runs each week; a speed workout, a tempo run, and a long run. The other adjustment he made to his training was the addition of a running journal. After each run, Todd would write down his distance, time/pace, the course he ran, and general notes on how the run went. His notes would include anything from how he felt at certain points of each run, to what he ate the night before or morning of each run, to the description of the course he ran. After his first long run, Todd had experienced some painful gastrointestinal issues that actually cut his run short for the day, which can be quite dissatisfying to runners who otherwise feel great physically. After his second long run, Todd had no discomfort at all. This pattern of stomach issue versus no stomach issue occurred on and off during the first four weeks of training. After taking a closer look at his journal, Todd made an interesting discovery.

Any time Todd experienced stomach issues on a long run, he had eaten chicken and brown rice the previous night. Any time he had no stomach discomfort, he had eaten sushi the night before. This seemingly inconsequential observation wound up paying major dividends for the remainder of his training. The night before every long run, it became Todd's new routine to eat three sushi rolls with a side order of sushi rice. He no longer had to worry about the painful stomach cramps that had plagued him in previous years. Further, he believed that the protein in the fish and the carbohydrates from the rice were the perfect balance for him. Whether this is true or not from a nutritional standpoint is up for debate. What was not debatable was how the food made him feel. And as we know, how we think and how we feel can play a significant role in how we perform.

So as you can see, the use of a running journal not only allowed for a change in eating habits for Todd, but it also shed light on his ability to achieve his daily and weekly goals. Keeping track of pace and distance for speed workouts, tempo runs, and the long runs constantly pushed Todd to meet or exceed these times on subsequent runs. This degree of organization and discipline resulted in Todd achieving a personal best at the Chicago Marathon.

A template for your journal is provided in **(Appendix B)**. Todd was kind enough to share most of the entries from his journal for this book **(see Appendix C)**. Remember, these are the actual thoughts, observations and conclusions from a real runner. There are two critical points I want to highlight with Todd's journal: (1) due to pre-planned commitments, Todd was unable to get in the three specific training runs recommended for each week. I stress this point because it illustrates that it is acceptable and typical to miss a day of training here or there and not try to make up for it by running more miles than your training program calls for or trying to squeeze in back-to-back runs for no productive reason; and (2) you'll notice his honesty in his descriptions of each run. It is this type of candor that allowed him to build confidence, make necessary changes, and ultimately have a peak performance on marathon day. Make it a point to record all the relevant information for each of your training runs as you experience all the many peaks and valleys associated with training.

After learning, practicing and integrating all of these mental skills, techniques and strategies, it is up to you to figure out the best way to utilize them come marathon day. The following list of 26 positive self-statements can serve as instant reminders of how you need to think and feel to run your best. Take them as is or feel free to tweak them to fit your style. The more you read them, the more you will believe them. And you can only achieve what you believe!

26 Positive Self-Statements

On Marathon Day I will...

1. Rise to the challenge when adversity comes my way.

2. Have the confidence needed to succeed.

3. Take charge of my feelings and maintain my emotions.

4. Have a game plan to keep me focused on what I have to do.

5. Think about the little things that make me a great runner.

6. Run my best and be satisfied with what I have accomplished.

7. Accept setbacks but not expect setbacks.

8. Visualize myself performing up to my potential.

9. Push myself by identifying challenging and realistic goals.

10. Utilize my routines to relax, focus and stay in the moment.

11. Take some time before and during the race to collect my thoughts and strategize for success.

12. Give 100% maximum physical and mental effort.

13. Be aware that my nerves are a sign that I am excited and ready to run.

14. Find time before the race to practice some deep breathing to help relax.

15. Keep my self-talk positive before and during the run.

16. Change negative thoughts like "I can't" to "I will."

17. Be tougher than the marathon.

18. Focus on my expectations for the marathon; not on what others want me to do or what I think others want me to accomplish.

19. Focus on tasks that are within my control.

20. View any stressful situation as a challenge.

21. Enjoy the experience of running the marathon.

22. Think, focus and react in a confident manner at all times.

23. Control my thoughts, feelings and performance.

24. Take responsibility for any and all successes and failures.

25. Run to the best of my abilities.

26. Believe in myself.

"Success will happen when I choose to think successfully!"

INTERMISSION: MENTAL HEALING

Throughout your training you will experience nagging little injuries. Hopefully these minor annoyances will not amount to anything substantial. Being mindful and aware of any injuries at their onset can save you valuable days and weeks if you address the problem early. However, there is always the chance that a freak injury occurs which seems to appear out of nowhere. Runners are at a loss for a reasonable explanation as to why they felt great one day and a horribly sharp pain in their foot the next. These injuries do not come out of nowhere. Proper strengthening and stretching exercises can certainly minimize injuries but it is also likely that something has been going on in your body for quite some time and it was that last run that finally caused a fracture in your foot, your IT band to tighten up, or your knee to throb. Many of the mental skills discussed in the first part of this book can also help you cope and survive your injuries. The following chapter gives you a little more insight into the psychology behind injuries as well as some specific strategies to help you mentally heal and overcome these physical setbacks as you ready yourself for the marathon.

CHAPTER 9: THE INJURY BUG

"I dropped four flights and cracked my spine, honey come quick with the iodine"

With all the good things that happen in running we sometimes ignore the harsh realities that come with the territory. Coping with injuries is a very real part of running and becomes a major psychological hurdle for many runners. If a runner suffers a serious injury they may experience elevated levels of self-doubt, anxiety, worry, despair, depression, and isolation. Runners want to believe that they are invincible so they sometimes ignore the warning signs of injury. Getting injured does not imply fragility or weakness. Fighting through legitimate physical pain may make you feel like a warrior today but you could be paying for it tomorrow. You only have an infinite amount of time from Day 1 of training to marathon day. Therefore, it is beyond critical to listen to your body and avoid a long-term injury. Runners typically go through the following 5 step process when they become injured.

1. **Denial:** Ignoring the seriousness of the injury and still trying to run through the pain which makes things worse.

2. **Anger:** Having the 'why me, why now' attitude and acting resentful to coaches, trainers, friends, and family.

3. **Bargaining:** Making deals with themselves that if they do 'this' then perhaps they can come back sooner.

4. **Depression:** Upon realizing how serious the injury is runners may experience sadness, low energy, and difficulty sleeping and eating. They go through a phase of hopelessness and loneliness.

5. **Acceptance:** After the runner finally accepts their situation they put it all into perspective and make the best of it. Even though they may not be able to run they can find alternative training methods until they get healthy.

There is no substitute for physical rehabilitation but the types of thoughts an injured runner has regarding their injury can have an effect on the rehabilitation process. It is common for runners to engage in excessive distorted negative self-talk during the early phase of recovery. Typical thoughts may include:

♦ I am never going to get back to where I was
♦ Why did this have to happen now; things were going so well
♦ This is just my luck, I can't seem to catch a break

Engaging in positive self-talk can help with confidence and adherence to the rehabilitation. Optimistic and hopeful thoughts of an injured runner include:

♦ I will be back soon if I continue to work hard
♦ With every day that goes by I am one day closer to my return
♦ I know that my exercises are making me stronger

Coming back from injury does not happen alone. Having strong social support from your family, friends, trainers, and doctors will help you physically and emotionally. Keep an open mind to what they have to say as well as to the following suggestions:

♦ Follow your doctor's advice closely. They have more experience with your injury than you do so listen to what they have to say.

♦ Remind yourself that your strong work ethic has helped you become a strong runner. Take the same approach to your rehab.

♦ Healing takes time so learn to be patient. Just because you are feeling better does not mean that you are healed. One step forward might mean two steps backwards if you try to come back too early.

♦ Once healthy, continue with proper exercise and stretching to remain injury-free.

♦ When coming back from your injury it is normal to be nervous or fearful of re-injury. Believing that bad things will happen due to a lack of conditioning can cause you to lack confidence and run tentatively. Maintain a positive mental attitude and focus on why you will be even stronger when you return to the streets.

♦ Regardless of how dedicated you are to your training, if your body has suffered a severe injury, you may have to put the marathon on hold. Remember, you will only have one body to train so make sure it is healthy. There will always be another marathon to train for.

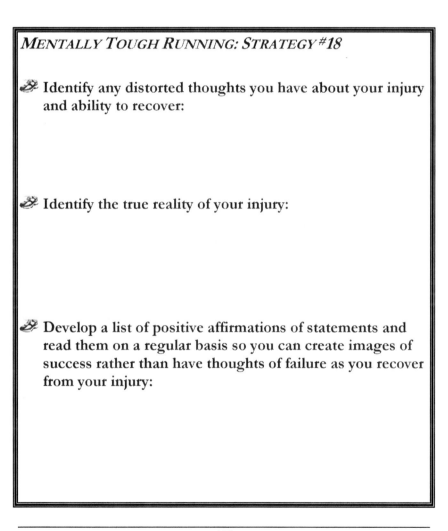

MENTALLY TOUGH RUNNING: STRATEGY #18

Identify any distorted thoughts you have about your injury and ability to recover:

Identify the true reality of your injury:

Develop a list of positive affirmations of statements and read them on a regular basis so you can create images of success rather than have thoughts of failure as you recover from your injury:

SET II: A GRATEFUL MARATHON EXPERIENCE

There is a famous axiom among Deadheads – "There's nothing like a Grateful Dead concert." I had the good fortune of seeing the Dead perform 15 times and I remember each show like it happened yesterday. Over the years, I have seen numerous bands and an abundance of concerts, but nothing has ever or will ever produce the same sense of thrill that a Grateful Dead show provided. Going to see the Dead is similar to running a marathon. After you see your first show or finish your first marathon, you are hooked. You want more. You want to learn as much as you can about why this event takes you to a place no other event could ever take you. You want to experience it again and again. Going to any other concert (while exciting in its own right) just does not produce the same electrifying emotions as a Grateful Dead show. After finishing 26.2 miles, running the local 5K just seems to be lacking the same buzz, energy and gratification the marathon provides. It's still great to cross the finish line, but the sense of achievement just isn't as grand. Simply put, there is nothing like running a marathon.

So what is the connection? In both cases, you are embarking on a journey that is full of anticipation, surprise, improvisation and absolute wonderment; an event that is beyond description. As the Dead would take the stage, there was a 'moment' right before they began playing. You knew where you were, you knew what was happening, the band would tune-up, and the lead up to the show hit an indescribable peak. Your excitement could not be contained. When you line up in your corral for the start of the marathon, the 'moment' occurs when the race official counts down to the start of the race. When the gun goes off you know you are in for the ride (or run) of your life.

One never knew what they would hear at a Dead show, just like one never knows what will happen the day of the marathon. The Dead were known to take risks on stage and improvise on the spot by playing a familiar song in a different tempo, or performing a song live for the first time with no rehearsal. Running the marathon is filled with constant improvisation. You have the plan of how you'd like the day to go but you must be willing to deviate and take chances to get to the finish line.

At the end of a Grateful Dead concert, when Jerry would play his last note and sing his final word, you were left with a sense of astonishment and amazement. You knew you were witness to something truly special and unique. And when you cross the finish line of your marathon, you will realize that you have just accomplished something truly extraordinary and remarkable.

The Grateful Dead and the marathon experience have changed the lives of hundreds of thousands of people. Just spend a few minutes with a Deadhead or a runner and they will explain how these events led them to lucid self-reflection and discovery in all areas of their life. But to truly understand it, you need to experience the phenomenon for yourself. And since the Grateful Dead are no more, it is the marathon that will help you realize genuine self-fulfillment.

So what can you expect as the marathon approaches? What will be going through your mind over the last few weeks? What will you be feeling? The following narrative, highlighted by the lyrics of the Grateful Dead, will give you both a balanced perspective and a sense of what a runner will typically experience as they propel themselves toward one of the single greatest personal and athletic achievements of their lives.

CHAPTER 10: 26.2 MILES DEAD AHEAD

The Two-Week Taper

"Stephen prospered in his time, well he may, and he may decline"

The final two weeks of training can be the most exciting yet stress-producing time during the training process. Many runners believe these final few weeks are also the most important. Throughout the duration of your training, you will be putting your body through intense training sessions that often lead to fatigue and loss of muscular strength. To perform at your peak, you need to train hard, but you also need to train smart. You want to give your body a chance to heal from the stress of those long runs, tempo runs, speed workouts and hill repeats. This is why the final two weeks of training, known as 'tapering,' are so critically vital to your overall success. The taper is part of every training program and is arguably the one aspect of training that should not be tinkered with. It serves as a break period for both your body and mind. A proper taper should allow your body adequate time to rest, repair and restore its energy in order to help you prepare for your upcoming marathon. Runners should heed the 'less is more' mindset during this time. While this sounds simple enough, many fastidious and persnickety runners have an extremely difficult time accepting this mentality.

The taper period does not eliminate your running, it lessens your running. You still continue your training but at a far reduced volume. This will keep you sharp yet, more importantly, energized for your race. It can be very difficult 'training down' the two weeks prior to your race since you are so accustomed to 'training up' for the past four or five months. So the taper can be far more of a mental challenge than physical challenge for runners. It is not uncommon for many runners to think they are 'losing what they gained' through their training and never take the needed break. It is a physiological fact that less training is needed to maintain previous gains than was originally needed to attain them. So remember and repeat the following sentence when you start convincing yourself you are out of shape in the days leading up to the marathon: "Tapering **does not** lead to a loss of conditioning."

The negative thoughts you may be having during the taper are normal so do not let them freak you out. What you want to do is shift your thought process from why something can't happen or what could go wrong, to all the things you have done well during your training runs and why the taper will be beneficial. Constantly remind yourself that the reduction in training is allowing your body to physically recover and mentally recharge, which will make you that much more enthused, inspired and prepared to run your marathon.

Marathon Eve

"The night comes so quiet and it's close on the heels of the day"

The days leading up to the marathon are filled with both excitement and apprehension. Every little ache you feel will be magnified and exaggerated a hundred times. You may find yourself questioning your level of fitness, the quality of your taper, and your ability to actually run the marathon. These thoughts and feelings are normal for all runners. There is absolutely nothing you can change about your training at this point, so just acknowledge these distorted perceptions and put them in your mental trash can.

Anything that can cause unwarranted stress should be avoided. For example, many runners will have friends and family coming to watch them run. You can help plan the itinerary in the weeks leading up to the marathon, but this weekend is all about you. Your focus needs to be on your preparation for the big day, not placating everyone else.

One part of the festivities of marathon weekend is the race exposition. It is here that runners pick up their official race number, timing chip and other assorted goodies. There are hundreds of vendors selling the latest in apparel, nutrition and training, as well as thousands of runners learning all they can about the newest products. The expo will certainly boost your anticipation of the race. You have never been around so many people sharing one common trait. Everywhere you turn there is something to remind you of the marathon. Even though the expo can serve as a time for runner bonding, keep in mind the goal – to be ready for marathon day. If it is at all possible, attend the expo two days before your race. This way you are not leaving anything to chance. You can take care of logistical business in advance and use the day prior to the race as your time to relax, reflect and prepare.

The good news is that your training is done and you are ready to run. The hard part is behind you and now it is time to reap the benefits of your training. The bad news is you probably won't have your best night's sleep the night before the race. So don't worry about it. Every thought you have will center on the race and no matter how positive or negative they are they will keep your mind racing. But let's get back to the good news – regardless of how much sleep you get the night before the marathon, your adrenaline will more than make up for it when you are out on the course. And I promise you will sleep like a baby after the race. Get all of your planning done now because before you know it, marathon eve will be here.

The key to feeling well rested is to get a good night sleep *two* nights before the race. So if you are running your marathon Sunday morning, get a good night's sleep Friday night. Simply take it easy on Saturday and stay off your feet as much as possible.

There are two common trouble areas for runners the day and evening before the marathon. First, you may hear about some runners getting in a few miles the day before the marathon, but let me assure you – it will not make you any more or any less trained. What it will do is make you more prone to the risk of a freak injury. Remember, you have trained your body to successfully run 26.2 miles, so relax it before you tax it.

Second, many people, including the media, will make it a point to inform runners to "eat a lot of pasta" for dinner the night before the race. Do not cave in to media pressure! Again, stick to your routine at this point. Whatever you eat the night before a typical long run is what you should eat the night before the marathon. This is your time to stay in your comfort zone and do what is most familiar to you. As I said before, you'll be tossing and turning all night with anticipation for the race. So the last thing you need to worry about is whether or not your unfamiliar meal will wreak havoc on your gastrointestinal tract. Eat your choice of dinner; perhaps take in a movie on your couch; double check to make sure you have everything laid out for the morning; take one last look at the weather to ensure you are properly prepared for the conditions; and just as you are about to call it a night, spend a few minutes visualizing the race as you lie in bed. Create the expectation of success for marathon day.

Marathon Morning

"Wake up to find out that you are the eyes of the world"

If you are lucky, you probably had about five hours of sleep. Shockingly though, you will not feel the least bit tired when you awake. If you have followed your routine, you should have marathon morning already planned out. Your race number should be pinned to your shirt or shorts, your racing chip properly affixed to your shoe, and your pre- and post-race wardrobe packed up and ready to go. Take a nice hot shower and utilize this time wisely. Think about your goals and begin to visualize the day. See everything unfold the way you anticipate it should. Eat your normal breakfast, drink your normal fluids, and listen to your favorite music. Do whatever you need to do to feel prepared to run. Take pause in the fact that you are about to experience something bigger than anything you have ever been involved in. Your marathon allows for a unique opportunity. You will never have the chance to take a swing against a major league pitcher, make a tackle against a professional football player, or score a basket in an NBA game. But today, for possibly the only time in your life, you will compete in an athletic competition with professional athletes. Today is going to be an extraordinary day so enjoy it, as the eyes of the world are on you.

Some marathons require you to take public transportation to the start. Other marathons allow you to drive yourself. However you choose to travel, make sure you give yourself plenty of time. You never know what traffic will be like in the morning or what unforeseen quandary you may face. Feeling rushed when getting to the race is not the way you want to start the day. If possible, try to arrive at the race at least 2-3 hours in advance. I know this may seem like a long time to sit around, but many marathons have plenty of things to occupy your time once you are there. Further, the extra downtime can play to your benefit as you can relax and continue to think about your goals for the day.

When you do arrive at your marathon destination, find an area where you can set up shop. Depending on how much time you have before the race begins, you may want to bring a little food or water with you. You will also have your race bag that should contain a change of clothes, shoes, and few other odds and ends. There will be a secure designated area for your baggage. Make sure you drop off your belongings well before the race starts because, again, stressing out about something as trivial as this is certainly not needed at this point.

Miles 1-10

"You know it's gonna get stranger, so let's get on with the show"

As the hours and minutes tick away to showtime, your nerves are sure to build up. You will meet many strangers in the athlete's village and hear some pretty bizarre marathon stories – some good and some not so good. While the anecdotes may be entertaining, take them at face value. Everyone has horror stories they like to share, but do not let them influence you. The race is about to begin and you have no idea what will unfold along the way. It is going to be a long and crazy day so try to stay focused, relaxed, and positive as you wait for the gun to go off and the race to start.

The first couple miles of the race are your time to take a moment and enjoy the experience. Thousands of runners are beginning their journey so take this opportunity to soak it all in. If you are at the back of the pack, it may take you anywhere from 10-20 minutes to cross the actual starting line. This delay will not affect your finishing time, as your starting time does not begin until you actually cross the starting line. This is why you have that chip on your sneaker. Many first-time marathoners, and even some veterans, will let their emotions get the better of them and come out too strong and too fast the first few miles. If you think you might be running too fast, *YOU ARE RUNNING TOO FAST*. This is a great time for you to incorporate some instructional self-talk – "Slow and steady" is a great mantra to repeat to yourself to ensure that you come out at an easy pace.

Some of you may run with a friend, some of you may run in a group, and some of you may be running by yourself. Try to find your groove in the first 10 miles of the race. I cannot stress how tempted you'll be to run fast during this time. The event itself, the crowd, and the other runners can make even the most disciplined runner break from their game plan. If you simplify the marathon into distinct components – the first 10 miles, the second 10 miles, and the last 6 miles (or some variation thereof) – you will find it much easier to stay in the moment. Instead of thinking about what will happen at mile 17, you will be focused on getting to mile 10 and then reassessing. Many first-time marathoners will fight a mental challenge when their mileage covered is still in the single digits, as the finish still seems so far away. It can be quite intimidating when you have been running for over an hour and still have nearly 20 miles to go. But once you reach double-digit mileage, something just seems to click and your confidence rises to a new level. It is also important to avoid the 'finishing time game'. Just because you feel strong the first 6 or 7 miles, do not make the leap to assume you will maintain that same pace for the entire marathon and run your personal best. Keep your thoughts in the moment. The more you focus on the process of running well, the better chance you have of obtaining that personal best.

Miles 11-19

"When life looks like easy street there is danger at your door"

At this point in the marathon you should have a steady pace going and you may have an urge to push it. Take this time to 'check-in' with yourself. How does your body feel? Can you run a little faster or do you need to slow things down a bit? Think about the rest of the course. Is it going to be hilly or flat? Resist temptation and think with your head, not with your heart. The goal is to finish so think about how you need to run, how often you need to hydrate, and when you need something to eat. After you pass the 13.1 mile marker, remember that you still have 13.1 miles to go. So don't change gears too soon. Save enough gas for the end of the race. I have seen many runners bonk out around mile 18 or 19. These runners came out way too fast in the beginning and tried to maintain that same pace throughout the race. They felt really good those first few miles and assumed they could keep it up. Runners beware – when you feel like things are too easy, danger can be right around the corner. Avoid the trap of keeping up with other runners just because you think you should be running as fast as them. Stick to your game plan and your performance since it is the only thing you can control.

As your approach miles 15-16, the marathon will get challenging both physically and mentally. You will have been running for over two-and-a-half hours. Again, take the time to 'check-in' with yourself. Where are your thoughts? Are you associating or dissociating? Is it better for you to closely monitor your body or do you need to tune out and focus on what is around you? What type of mindset will help you the most at this point? Use your mind to help you through the challenges. You have the mental tools in your arsenal so take advantage of them. Many runners find mental comfort when they pass mile 17. It is at this point that the finish line is less than 10 miles away. The single-digit mileage is now working in your favor. But don't let your mind wander too far into the future, as the immediate goal is to make it to mile 20 and complete your 'second phase' of the marathon.

Mile 20

"Struggling man has got to move, struggling man no time to lose,
I'm a struggling man, and I've got to move on"

Many runners concur that the marathon does not really start until mile 20. For most first-time marathoners, anything beyond this distance is foreign territory since your longest training run typically caps at 20 miles. You really have no idea how your body will respond. The true mental toughness of a runner will be tested from this point on. With only six miles to the finish, you know you *can* do it, but you may not know *how* you are going to do it. Your body has been put through tremendous physical stress at this point. Twinges and cramping are shooting through muscles you never knew existed. But this is no time to dwell on the negatives. Think about how close you are to accomplishing your goal. Even though you are experiencing physical pain on a new level, you need to put it in perspective. Remind yourself that you chose to be in this physically and mentally challenging predicament. As uncomfortable as you may be, appreciate the fact that you are able to be out there on marathon day, pushing your body to new limits. There are many people who would give anything to be in your position. Believe it or not, they would trade places with you in a heartbeat just to be able to experience what running feels like. So in the big scheme of things, what's a little discomfort at this point?

Miles 21-24

"Death don't have no mercy in this land"

For the first-time marathoner, you are now entering mileage unfamiliar to your body. For the experienced marathoner, you may face some new challenge. Many runners have mentally and physically hit the wall at this point and they are running on sheer guts and willpower. Their mind says go but their body says no. The marathon shows you no mercy from this point on. Runners literally feel like death on two feet. As you battle through the mental and physical pain, it is crucial to control your thoughts so you can control the way you feel. Having the wherewithal to 'check-in' at this point can prove to be decisive to your finishing the race. Once you pass mile 23 you are three miles away from the finish. Think about it? How many 3-mile runs have you completed over the course of your training? Use these past performance accomplishments to mentally get you through each ensuing mile. Forget about the fact you have been running for 23 miles. Simply think of it as a 3-mile run, or perhaps, three 1-mile runs. With the finish line right around the corner, some runners like to play the 'pick-off' game. This is where they find a runner a little bit ahead of them, make them their target and focus their energies on passing that runner. By thinking about the next runner you want to pick off, your mind is in the present which will help you focus for the final stretch. However you break down the final leg of the marathon, think about the process of finishing. Utilize your affirmations, mantras or trigger words. As hard as it may seem, dominate your thoughts with success. The marathon might be tough, but you are tougher than the marathon!

Mile 25

"Keep a rolling, just a mile to go, keep on rolling, my old buddy you're moving much too slow"

You are just over a mile away from finishing. There is a good chance you are starting to feel the euphoria that is soon to come. Do not stray too far into the future because the race is not quite over. Stay focused on this mile and not the finish line. As you see the sign for mile 26 control your excitement as you still have two-tenths of a mile to go. I know this does not seem like much but trust me on this. The final two-tenths of a mile may feel longer than the first 26.

The stretch between mile 25 and 26 of the marathon can be very emotional for a runner. It offers you a time to reflect on what you just did. Think about how far you have come over the past four or five months. You set a goal, worked hard, and did whatever you had to do to achieve your goal. You may have dealt with an array of setbacks, injuries and challenges during both your training and this marathon – but you had the mental toughness to cope and overcome them all. Hundreds of thoughts and images will flash before you as you approach the finish line. Embrace this moment. You may never experience it again.

Mile 26.2

"This must be heaven, last station on the line"

Believe it or not, you just crossed the finish line. The one place on earth you probably thought you would never reach just a few hours ago. No matter how long it took you to finish, you did finish the marathon and that is all that counts. You will now realize why the marathon is such a special event. You accomplished something truly amazing. Make sure you receive your finisher's medal, grab something to eat and drink, stretch, and have a moment to yourself. Wear your medal proudly as you are no longer a marathon runner; you are a now a marathoner.

Now that you have finished and can finally stop running, find your race bag, take off your sneakers, pull off your shirt, and change into some dry, comfortable clothes. It is wise to keep moving at this point, too. Although you are physically and mentally spent, and the thought of lying face down on concrete seems strangely appealing, you want to keep your body moving so it does not cramp up.

So now that you are done, what do you do? Well, after completing the marathon, some runners may choose to stick around the finish line and cheer on the other runners as they come in. Some will seek out a complimentary massage. Others simply want to get home and call it a day. Regardless of what you do, drink in the atmosphere (among other things). And as promised, you will have a wonderful night's sleep.

"Going home, going home, by the waterside I will rest my bones, listen to the river sing sweet songs, to rock my soul"

ENCORE: THE END OR BEGINNING?

After spending 4-5 months dedicating every waking moment to your marathon training – plus going through the euphoria, elation and jubilation of marathon weekend and the race itself – many runners may find themselves feeling empty, unfocused, irritable and depressed. Is this normal? Why does it happen? What can you do to keep a healthy perspective on running during your off-season?

Yes, it is completely normal to feel a sense of emptiness and depression following your race. Whenever we put a lot of time and effort into an activity and have such high expectations for an event, we are bound to be at a loss for what to do with ourselves when it is over. We forget what it's like to have a free Saturday or Sunday when running 15 miles is no longer the priority. We forget how it feels to go out and have a few drinks on the weekend and not worry about missing an early morning long run.

What is it about completing a marathon that can take a runner from feeling so exhilarated and accomplished to feeling so adrift and despondent? For many first-time runners, training for a marathon is the first time in a while (maybe ever) that they've held themselves accountable to a structured training regimen. Never before have they disciplined themselves to train with a specific goal in mind. Now that the goal has been achieved, where else is there to go?

The key to overcoming this sense of loss is to find a new activity or hobby to occupy your time. As training begins to wind down, many runners will begin thinking of their next challenge to help them deal with the imminent end of their current event. Some runners may be thinking more about how sore their body is from the marathon than what their next marathon will be. But give yourself a few weeks to recover and you'll be craving the regulation and organization that defined your life just a short time ago. Whatever path you choose to pursue, you need to ask yourself the following question – "What new challenge will make me feel really good about myself?" Many runners find the answer to be simple – train for another marathon. Typically with the next race a runner will raise the stakes. A first-timer is no longer happy just to finish, they want to improve their time. And a competitive runner is no longer satisfied with their time…now they want to run a qualifying time. Some runners may want the experience of running one of the bigger races, like Boston, New York or Chicago.

Although you may be highly motivated to tackle the next challenge, take an appropriate amount of time to recover before moving on. Immediately jumping into the fire increases the risk of physical injury and mental burnout. Maintaining a positive outlook during your off-time will allow you to clearly evaluate your previous training methods; identify what worked well for you; recognize how you can improve your running and training habits; and isolate the steps you need to take to make those improvements happen.

Whatever your goal may be, the mere fact that you have taken the time to think about what it is you'd like to do next is most significant. You will regain a sense of control and structure over your life, and feel motivated, happy and focused as you push yourself to an even higher level of personal and athletic achievement.

"Truckin', I'm a going home, whoa whoa baby back where I belong. Back home, sit back and patch my bones, and get back truckin' on"

POSTSCRIPT: GO FURTHER

My intention for this book was to shed light on the mental skills that all successful athletes utilize to achieve peak performance on command. It is up to you to master these strategies as you apply them to your marathon training. For some people, the marathon will be a one-time experience that will last a lifetime. For others, it will become a lifetime endeavor fulfilled every year. Regardless of how your story unfolds, take the time to appreciate your accomplishment. Train and run without regret. As peculiar as this may sound, the marathon allows you the opportunity to forget all the hassles and stress of everyday life. Enjoy the marathon for the enriching and inspirational experience it provides. Use this life-changing event as a springboard to advance your personal and professional activities. Having the motivation, structure, imagination, attitude, poise, awareness and mental toughness to train for and finish a marathon are powerful personal attributes you will always be able to depend on when faced with the challenges life is bound to throw your way.

"Oh well, a touch a gray kind of suits you anyway, that was all I had to say and that's alright"

~GTK

APPENDIX A
Weekly Goal-Setting Sheets

The following goal-setting sheets are for you to complete on a weekly basis. At the beginning of each week, think about what you'd like to accomplish for each run and workout. Your goals may be based on recommended mileage, successes or failures encountered the prior week, or any other physical, mental, nutritional, athletic or personal pursuits you may have.

You will notice that there are 6 days per week for you to identify your goals. This was done purposely as you should take at least 1 day off per week to let your body and mind recover.

The overall purpose for your goal setting is to feel a strong sense of accomplishment and achieve daily/weekly success as you progress through your marathon training.

1. *Identify ONE overall challenge for the week* – What do you want to do that will push you to achieve a new level of success?

2. *Identify process, performance, and outcome goals* – Set goals that challenge you to improve from the previous week. These could be both performance and outcome based.

3. *Identify potential roadblocks* – What could inhibit your ability to achieve your performance/process-oriented goals?

4. *Plan of attack* – Describe in detail your plan to overcome roadblocks and achieve your goals on a daily basis.

5. *Evaluation* – Identify the positives and negatives of each training session. Did you accomplish your goals or did you stumble? Identify 1 'feel good' moment to boost your confidence.

CHALLENGE FOR WEEK 1: _____

DAY 1: GOALS & ROADBLOCKS:

PLAN OF ATTACK:

EVALUATION:

DAY 2: GOALS & ROADBLOCKS:

PLAN OF ATTACK:

EVALUATION:

DAY 3: GOALS & ROADBLOCKS:

PLAN OF ATTACK:

EVALUATION:

DAY 4: GOALS & ROADBLOCKS:

PLAN OF ATTACK:

EVALUATION:

DAY 5: GOALS & ROADBLOCKS:

PLAN OF ATTACK:

EVALUATION:

DAY 6: GOALS & ROADBLOCKS:

PLAN OF ATTACK:

EVALUATION:

CHALLENGE FOR WEEK 2: _____

DAY 1: GOALS & ROADBLOCKS:

PLAN OF ATTACK:

EVALUATION:

DAY 2: GOALS & ROADBLOCKS:

PLAN OF ATTACK:

EVALUATION:

DAY 3: GOALS & ROADBLOCKS:

PLAN OF ATTACK:

EVALUATION:

DAY 4: GOALS & ROADBLOCKS:

PLAN OF ATTACK:

EVALUATION:

DAY 5: GOALS & ROADBLOCKS:

PLAN OF ATTACK:

EVALUATION:

DAY 6: GOALS & ROADBLOCKS:

PLAN OF ATTACK:

EVALUATION:

CHALLENGE FOR WEEK 3: _____

DAY 1: GOALS & ROADBLOCKS:

PLAN OF ATTACK:

EVALUATION:

DAY 2: GOALS & ROADBLOCKS:

PLAN OF ATTACK:

EVALUATION:

DAY 3: GOALS & ROADBLOCKS:

PLAN OF ATTACK:

EVALUATION:

DAY 4: GOALS & ROADBLOCKS:

PLAN OF ATTACK:

EVALUATION:

DAY 5: GOALS & ROADBLOCKS:

PLAN OF ATTACK:

EVALUATION:

DAY 6: GOALS & ROADBLOCKS:

PLAN OF ATTACK:

EVALUATION:

CHALLENGE FOR WEEK 4: _____

DAY 1: GOALS & ROADBLOCKS:

PLAN OF ATTACK:

EVALUATION:

DAY 2: GOALS & ROADBLOCKS:

PLAN OF ATTACK:

EVALUATION:

DAY 3: GOALS & ROADBLOCKS:

PLAN OF ATTACK:

EVALUATION:

DAY 4: GOALS & ROADBLOCKS:

PLAN OF ATTACK:

EVALUATION:

DAY 5: GOALS & ROADBLOCKS:

PLAN OF ATTACK:

EVALUATION:

DAY 6: GOALS & ROADBLOCKS:

PLAN OF ATTACK:

EVALUATION:

CHALLENGE FOR WEEK 5: _____

DAY 1: GOALS & ROADBLOCKS:

PLAN OF ATTACK:

EVALUATION:

DAY 2: GOALS & ROADBLOCKS:

PLAN OF ATTACK:

EVALUATION:

DAY 3: GOALS & ROADBLOCKS:

PLAN OF ATTACK:

EVALUATION:

DAY 4: GOALS & ROADBLOCKS:

PLAN OF ATTACK:

EVALUATION:

DAY 5: GOALS & ROADBLOCKS:

PLAN OF ATTACK:

EVALUATION:

DAY 6: GOALS & ROADBLOCKS:

PLAN OF ATTACK:

EVALUATION:

CHALLENGE FOR WEEK 6: _____

DAY 1: GOALS & ROADBLOCKS:

PLAN OF ATTACK:

EVALUATION:

DAY 2: GOALS & ROADBLOCKS:

PLAN OF ATTACK:

EVALUATION:

DAY 3: GOALS & ROADBLOCKS:

PLAN OF ATTACK:

EVALUATION:

DAY 4: GOALS & ROADBLOCKS:

PLAN OF ATTACK:

EVALUATION:

DAY 5: GOALS & ROADBLOCKS:

PLAN OF ATTACK:

EVALUATION:

DAY 6: GOALS & ROADBLOCKS:

PLAN OF ATTACK:

EVALUATION:

CHALLENGE FOR WEEK 7: _____

DAY 1: GOALS & ROADBLOCKS:

PLAN OF ATTACK:

EVALUATION:

DAY 2: GOALS & ROADBLOCKS:

PLAN OF ATTACK:

EVALUATION:

DAY 3: GOALS & ROADBLOCKS:

PLAN OF ATTACK:

EVALUATION:

DAY 4: GOALS & ROADBLOCKS:

PLAN OF ATTACK:

EVALUATION:

DAY 5: GOALS & ROADBLOCKS:

PLAN OF ATTACK:

EVALUATION:

DAY 6: GOALS & ROADBLOCKS:

PLAN OF ATTACK:

EVALUATION:

CHALLENGE FOR WEEK 8: _____

DAY 1: GOALS & ROADBLOCKS:

PLAN OF ATTACK:

EVALUATION:

DAY 2: GOALS & ROADBLOCKS:

PLAN OF ATTACK:

EVALUATION:

DAY 3: GOALS & ROADBLOCKS:

PLAN OF ATTACK:

EVALUATION:

DAY 4: GOALS & ROADBLOCKS:

PLAN OF ATTACK:

EVALUATION:

DAY 5: GOALS & ROADBLOCKS:

PLAN OF ATTACK:

EVALUATION:

DAY 6: GOALS & ROADBLOCKS:

PLAN OF ATTACK:

EVALUATION:

CHALLENGE FOR WEEK 9: _____

DAY 1: GOALS & ROADBLOCKS:

PLAN OF ATTACK:

EVALUATION:

DAY 2: GOALS & ROADBLOCKS:

PLAN OF ATTACK:

EVALUATION:

DAY 3: GOALS & ROADBLOCKS:

PLAN OF ATTACK:

EVALUATION:

DAY 4: GOALS & ROADBLOCKS:

PLAN OF ATTACK:

EVALUATION:

DAY 5: GOALS & ROADBLOCKS:

PLAN OF ATTACK:

EVALUATION:

DAY 6: GOALS & ROADBLOCKS:

PLAN OF ATTACK:

EVALUATION:

CHALLENGE FOR WEEK 10: _____

DAY 1: GOALS & ROADBLOCKS:

PLAN OF ATTACK:

EVALUATION:

DAY 2: GOALS & ROADBLOCKS:

PLAN OF ATTACK:

EVALUATION:

DAY 3: GOALS & ROADBLOCKS:

PLAN OF ATTACK:

EVALUATION:

DAY 4: GOALS & ROADBLOCKS:

PLAN OF ATTACK:

EVALUATION:

DAY 5: GOALS & ROADBLOCKS:

PLAN OF ATTACK:

EVALUATION:

DAY 6: GOALS & ROADBLOCKS:

PLAN OF ATTACK:

EVALUATION:

CHALLENGE FOR WEEK 11: _____

DAY 1: GOALS & ROADBLOCKS:

PLAN OF ATTACK:

EVALUATION:

DAY 2: GOALS & ROADBLOCKS:

PLAN OF ATTACK:

EVALUATION:

DAY 3: GOALS & ROADBLOCKS:

PLAN OF ATTACK:

EVALUATION:

DAY 4: GOALS & ROADBLOCKS:

PLAN OF ATTACK:

EVALUATION:

DAY 5: GOALS & ROADBLOCKS:

PLAN OF ATTACK:

EVALUATION:

DAY 6: GOALS & ROADBLOCKS:

PLAN OF ATTACK:

EVALUATION:

CHALLENGE FOR WEEK 12: _____

DAY 1: GOALS & ROADBLOCKS:

PLAN OF ATTACK:

EVALUATION:

DAY 2: GOALS & ROADBLOCKS:

PLAN OF ATTACK:

EVALUATION:

DAY 3: GOALS & ROADBLOCKS:

PLAN OF ATTACK:

EVALUATION:

DAY 4: GOALS & ROADBLOCKS:

PLAN OF ATTACK:

EVALUATION:

DAY 5: GOALS & ROADBLOCKS:

PLAN OF ATTACK:

EVALUATION:

DAY 6: GOALS & ROADBLOCKS:

PLAN OF ATTACK:

EVALUATION:

CHALLENGE FOR WEEK 13: _____

DAY 1: GOALS & ROADBLOCKS:

PLAN OF ATTACK:

EVALUATION:

DAY 2: GOALS & ROADBLOCKS:

PLAN OF ATTACK:

EVALUATION:

DAY 3: GOALS & ROADBLOCKS:

PLAN OF ATTACK:

EVALUATION:

DAY 4: GOALS & ROADBLOCKS:

PLAN OF ATTACK:

EVALUATION:

DAY 5: GOALS & ROADBLOCKS:

PLAN OF ATTACK:

EVALUATION:

DAY 6: GOALS & ROADBLOCKS:

PLAN OF ATTACK:

EVALUATION:

CHALLENGE FOR WEEK 14: _____

DAY 1: GOALS & ROADBLOCKS:

PLAN OF ATTACK:

EVALUATION:

DAY 2: GOALS & ROADBLOCKS:

PLAN OF ATTACK:

EVALUATION:

DAY 3: GOALS & ROADBLOCKS:

PLAN OF ATTACK:

EVALUATION:

DAY 4: GOALS & ROADBLOCKS:

PLAN OF ATTACK:

EVALUATION:

DAY 5: GOALS & ROADBLOCKS:

PLAN OF ATTACK:

EVALUATION:

DAY 6: GOALS & ROADBLOCKS:

PLAN OF ATTACK:

EVALUATION:

CHALLENGE FOR WEEK 15: _____

DAY 1: GOALS & ROADBLOCKS:

PLAN OF ATTACK:

EVALUATION:

DAY 2: GOALS & ROADBLOCKS:

PLAN OF ATTACK:

EVALUATION:

DAY 3: GOALS & ROADBLOCKS:

PLAN OF ATTACK:

EVALUATION:

DAY 4: GOALS & ROADBLOCKS:

PLAN OF ATTACK:

EVALUATION:

DAY 5: GOALS & ROADBLOCKS:

PLAN OF ATTACK:

EVALUATION:

DAY 6: GOALS & ROADBLOCKS:

PLAN OF ATTACK:

EVALUATION:

CHALLENGE FOR WEEK 16: _____

DAY 1: GOALS & ROADBLOCKS:

PLAN OF ATTACK:

EVALUATION:

DAY 2: GOALS & ROADBLOCKS:

PLAN OF ATTACK:

EVALUATION:

DAY 3: GOALS & ROADBLOCKS:

PLAN OF ATTACK:

EVALUATION:

DAY 4: GOALS & ROADBLOCKS:

PLAN OF ATTACK:

EVALUATION:

DAY 5: GOALS & ROADBLOCKS:

PLAN OF ATTACK:

EVALUATION:

DAY 6: GOALS & ROADBLOCKS:

PLAN OF ATTACK:

EVALUATION:

MARATHON CHALLENGE:

I WILL ACHIEVE A NEW LEVEL OF SUCCESS TODAY BY...

_____

OUTCOME GOAL FOR THE MARATHON:

PERFORMANCE & PROCESS GOALS THAT WILL HELP ME REACH MY OUTCOME GOAL:

1. _____

2. _____

POTENTIAL ROADBLOCKS: Identify 2-3 potential roadblocks that could hinder your ability to meet the challenge of the marathon:

1. _____

2. _____

3. _____

PLAN OF ATTACK: How will you overcome these roadblocks and achieve your goals? What specific steps will you take to be successful on Marathon Day?

APPENDIX B

Running Journal Template

1. Keep track of your distance for each run.

2. Identify which mental strategies you used prior to and during each run.

3. Rate your performance from a physical (*mechanics, speed, endurance, strength, pace*) and mental *(motivation, feeling confident, proud, high effort level, positive thoughts, specific goals, focus, handling nerves)* perspective.

4. Summarize your day. What went well, what didn't go well, what changes/improvements do you need to make?

5. Use the following template to record your results.

DATE	DISTANCE	TIME	COURSE

Notes:

APPENDIX C
Running Journal

Note: *As an experienced runner who had been incorporating mental skills into his training for years, Todd did not include the specific mental strategies used during his runs in his comments.*

DATE	DISTANCE	TIME	COURSE
4-Jul	2x1600m 1x800m	6:54, 6:51 3:21	Clemente Track

NOTES:

Supposed to do 3x1600 but opted for 2.5 sets instead. Pushed hard, gave max effort on all three sets. Legs felt strong for the most part, no nagging aches/pains – good run overall.

DATE	DISTANCE	TIME	COURSE
6-Jul	6 miles	47:55 7:58/pace	BC Reservoir

NOTES:

Bloated, gassy, but felt good, right quad sore. Hit my goal time.

DATE	DISTANCE	TIME	COURSE
8-Jul	13 miles	1:45:45 8:08/pace	Charles

NOTES:

Ran at a good pace, a bit quicker than what the schedule asks, but felt fine. Started to get cramps in lower stomach 4-5 miles in – not too bad until the last few miles. Right quad still sore – need to stretch that out.

DATE	DISTANCE	TIME	COURSE
10-Jul	4x800m	3:19, 3:15 3:15, 3:21	MIT Track

NOTES:

Strong run, very hot, repeats 2&3 were very strong – felt fast. Last repeat was tough and certainly felt maxed by the end. Legs felt strong, no soreness. Breathing was deep and shallow during run.

DATE	DISTANCE	TIME	COURSE
12-Jul	7 miles	54:48 7:50/pace	Beacon St to Chestnut Hill Ave to Comm Ave to Beacon St Loop

NOTES:

Strong run, maintained 8-min pace majority of time. No soreness in legs, breathing was deep, not forced. Weather was pretty warm, slightly humid.

DATE	DISTANCE	TIME	COURSE
15-Jul	15 miles	2:06:05 8:24/pace	Beacon St to Amory to Comm Ave to BU Bridge Loop to Comm to Beacon

NOTES:

Another strong run. Legs felt fine the whole time, stomach did not cramp. First run with fuel belt – one Powerade and one water. Had gummy bears but did not eat them. Never felt dehydrated but was a little taxed by mile 13. Ran the final mile at a strong clip – felt good to be able to pick it up a notch toward the end.

DATE	DISTANCE	TIME	COURSE
18-Jul	1200, 1000, 800, 600, 400, 200	Within 5 sec of goal pace each distance	MIT Track

NOTES:

Started at 8 a.m. and it was already getting steamy. Had a Z-bar for breakfast, felt a tiny bit hungry but did not affect the run. Took a slow 12-minute warm-up followed by the repeats. First 1200 felt a little rough but was strong on the 1000, 800, 600. Felt a bit gassed and had trouble really turning it on for the one-lap and half-lap, although I finished under the goal pace/time.

DATE	DISTANCE	TIME	COURSE
20-Jul	7 miles	52:15 7:27/pace	Beacon St to Chestnut Hill Ave to Comm Ave to Beacon St Loop

NOTES:

Cool weather this morning which made for a pleasant run. Did not eat dinner last night – stuffed from trail mix – but had a Clif Bar about 2 hours before the run. Felt like I had enough gas in the tank, was not bloated. Could have used a little more hydration pre-run but that's about it. Maintained prescribed pace for the entire run – felt strong throughout and was able to turn it on for the last mile. Good confidence builder for Saturday's 17 miler.

DATE	DISTANCE	TIME	COURSE
22-Jul	17 miles	2:25:38 8:34/pace	Beacon St to Comm Ave to BU Bridge to N Beacon to BU

NOTES:

Misty rain, slightly humid, but cool breeze coming off the Charles River. iPod nano wouldn't work, had to go with the Mini on the arm – not ideal but dealt with it. Had bagel and Clif Bar for breakfast. First 7 miles were great except headphones went out so took off iPod for final 10 miles which wasn't that bad – reminded me of 2002 training so I was prepared. Had fuel belt and jelly beans. Felt slight cramping around mile 11-12 and by 14, had to stop as the pressure in the belly was too much to run. Stopped my watch on these extended stops, so while my time was dead on with what I wanted, it is slightly skewed. Stopped again at mile 15.5 and the gas finally subsided and intense hunger kicked in for the final piece of the run. Wasn't my best finish but hadn't run this distance in about fifteen months. Legs were spent at the end, GI issues, felt a little nausea, but cardiovascular was tip-top. Above average run overall – may cut next week's 20 miler to 18.

DATE	DISTANCE	TIME	COURSE
25-Jul	5x1K	5 seconds of goal time	Clemente Track

NOTES:

Another hot day and did the run mid/late afternoon. Only did 3 laps on the track (2.5 times around) and did one 1000 meters before and after track to conserve time. Legs felt a bit heavy at times but I think the track may have played a role in that – had been on MIT the past few weeks. Speed is right where it should be, according to workouts.

DATE	DISTANCE	TIME	COURSE
27-Jul	5 miles	38:52 7:46/mile	BC Reservoir

NOTES:

Steamy hot day – started running a bit later than I had hoped. The first half-mile or so my watch was not on so I restarted my time and cut the run short by .5 miles. Felt like I was running out of gas, but ran the designated 4 miles at the proper pace. No stomach issues, felt strong in the upper body on the run – made a decision to cut back on weights – still 2 days a week but cutting back on number of exercises, etc. Feel that if I drop around 5 lbs between now and October, I'll be at my perfect running weight – 168-170 is the goal. Decided that Saturday will be an 18-20 miler with 18 being the true goal.

DATE	DISTANCE	TIME	COURSE
29-Jul	19 miles	2:43:22 8:36/pace	Beacon to Kenmore to St. Paul to BU to Arsenal to Comm Ave to St. Mary to Cool Corner

NOTES:

Started very early, around 6:20 to beat the heat – good idea! Wore a hat and had my fuel belt, along with sport beans. Ran about 4 miles, met up with Andrew and ran another 6 miles with him. Pace was dead-on, legs felt strong, heat was not yet an issue when I hit the 10-mile mark. At this point, I debated whether I would do 18, 19 or 20 miles. Sport beans were good, nice mix of water/Powerade, felt like my energy was high, although the heat came around and tried to bust me. Stomach was fine the whole run – a drastic improvement from last week. At no point did I feel any type of stomach pain which played a major role in the overall success of this run. Although I felt like I was tiring around mile 16-17, I made the decision to go 19 miles. My pace was still good, hovering in the high 8s/low 9s. I finished 18 miles when I got back to the BU footbridge, rested for less than a minute and walked to Comm Ave and ran the final mile to Coolidge Corner. My overall time was great, although I did stop the watch on these "extended" breaks – more interested with my actual running time as things should be cooler on race day.

DATE	DISTANCE	TIME	COURSE
15-Aug	6x800	Within 3-5 sec of goal time	St. Joseph's Track

NOTES:

Was in Hartford for work and luckily found a track. Ran late in the day, around 7 p.m., which is not ideal for me, but had no choice. After initial warm-up jog, I did a few active stretches and felt a slight twinge in left calf and it continued very minimally during the first 1 or 2 repeats. Overall, I was right within my goal time for each repeat and nailed the last one in my fastest time of the day. The music certainly helped but I kept visualizing the last few miles of the marathon and it made a significant difference in terms of my focus. Was nice to end on a strong note – one of better track workouts I had the past few weeks.

DATE	DISTANCE	TIME	COURSE
17-Aug	6 miles	47:05 7:51/pace	Beacon St to BC reservoir to Comm Ave to Beacon St

NOTES:

Was supposed to run 8 miles but did a late afternoon run and didn't feel at 100%. Calf was a bit tight during the first few miles and having to run at a quick pace, I didn't want to chance anything. About 4 miles in started getting stomach cramps, probably from lunch a few hours earlier and maybe the heat/lack of hydration. In the end, did 6 miles and still ran at a pace slightly faster than goal time. And if I had to, I could have done the last 2 miles. Big run this weekend, 18 miles, so I need to stretch the calf and will probably wear the neoprene sleeve as a precautionary measure.

DATE	DISTANCE	TIME	COURSE
19-Aug	18 miles	2:30:38 8:22/pace	Beacon St to Mass Ave to Amory to BU Bridge to Eliot Loop to Comm Ave to Kenmore to Beacon to Coolidge Corner

NOTES:

Started the run about 30 minutes later than planned. Wore the calf sleeve which alleviated pain/strain from the calf and actually helped with my Achilles. Sun was hot early on and I felt a bit "off," hoping it wouldn't steam up too quickly. When I got to the river, I had covered 6 miles and started to hit my groove but felt hungry and had a few bites of my Clif Bar. I made it a point to stop every 3 miles for water/Powerade. By mile 9, things felt fine, hydration was good, ate some sport beans and was halfway through the run. Next 3 miles seemed to go relatively quick and was able to maintain a low 8/pace. Miles 12-15 were not as bad as I thought they'd be, taking the heat/sun into consideration. Was within minutes of my time from last week when I hit mile 15 so that was a good confidence boost. Finished up at the river just over 16 miles, and then hit Comm Ave to Kenmore to Coolidge Corner for the final 2 miles. I definitely felt the added mileage at this point. Certainly felt like I worked hard today, but if push came to shove, I could have managed another 2 miles, albeit at a somewhat slower pace.

DATE	DISTANCE	TIME	COURSE
12-Sep	1K, 2K, 1K	on-time	Clemente Track

NOTES:

Warm weather today and the workout was a challenge but I actually felt fine physically the whole time. Crushed the 1K in targeted times and hit the 2K as well. Felt nice to run 1.25 miles in 8:20 or so…a little crunched for time so I bailed on the final 1K – no crises.

DATE	DISTANCE	TIME	COURSE
14-Sep	5.6	43:32 7:46/pace	Beacon St to Comm Ave to Beacon St

NOTES:

Weather was a tad warmer than I thought, but quite comfortable. A little crunched for time so I cut the run short by 4/10ths of a mile – no big deal. Body felt good, was cranking hard toward the end and was right on target pace.

DATE	DISTANCE	TIME	COURSE
16-Sep	18 miles	2:32:03 8:27/pace	Beacon to Commons to Comm Ave to Eliot Loop to Dartmouth to St. Paul

NOTES:

Solid run, good confidence booster. Had to make one pit stop about 7 miles in due to raisin bagel – need to stick with plain. Aside from that, no pain, no issues, etc. Kept watch going whole time except for the raisin stop. By the end, felt like I could have done 2 more miles, but wanted to play it smart and stick to the plan.

DATE	DISTANCE	TIME	COURSE
19-Sep	3x1600	6:42, 6:38, 6:40	Brookline Track

NOTES:

Used the Brookline track for the first time this summer as it just completed renovation. Very spongy and springy – a joy to run on. Did the full workout for the first time this training season and improved my times by nearly 15 seconds as compared to the first week of speed workouts. Great confidence booster that I could cut the time over the past few months. Felt a slight twinge in my left groin area the day prior but realized I wasn't fully recovered from Saturday's run to do this speed workout. Glad I held out and should be strong for Friday's 15-miler.

DATE	DISTANCE	TIME	COURSE
22-Sep	15 miles	2:05:37 8:23/pace	Beacon St to Dartmouth to River St Loop to Beacon St

NOTES:

Friday morning run – body not quite in tune with the day but found my groove around mile 6-7. Weather was nice and cool, low 50s to start so I didn't bring any water since I knew I would have three water fountains along the route. Hamstrings felt a little tight toward the end – may have had to do with reverse lunges from yesterday – no more of those! Was able to pick it up for the last mile which is always a good sign and my pace was right on target. One more long run next week and then it's taper time. Compared to my last marathon, I feel much better physically at this point which is another good sign.

DATE	DISTANCE	TIME	COURSE
26-Sep	10x400	1:30-1:34	Brookline Track

NOTES:

Early morning track workout. Did a 10 minute warm up and then started the 400m repeats. The first 4-6 were pretty good; I came in at 1:30 per lap. I only rested half-lap instead of a full due to time constraints – that may have had something to do with my times slowing down by 4-5 seconds on the final 3-4 laps. I stopped after 9 repeats as I had to go. My times were dead on with the projected pace. Looking forward to the 3 day run week.

DATE	DISTANCE	TIME	COURSE
28-Sep	7.5 miles	58:27 7:48/pace	Beacon St – Fairfield Loop

NOTES:

Planned to do 8 miles but again was crunched for time so I did 7.5. Ran it at a pace about 20 seconds quicker than projected. Can really feel the difference with running sub-8s for mid-distance and actually looking forward to slowing the pace by about 45 seconds for the 20-miler this weekend. Body feels good with 3+ weeks to go. Get through Saturday and I'm in the home stretch.

DATE	DISTANCE	TIME	COURSE
30-Sep	20 miles	2:50:26 8:31/pace	Beacon St to Commons to Charles River to Beacon St

NOTES:

Cool weather to start the run, probably low 50s. First few miles were normal, working out the kinks. Hit a groove between miles 5-8. Around mile 6, had first water break and a mile or so later, took a pee break. Made it a point to keep the watch moving the whole time. Hit the river at 8 miles and had two more water breaks by Eliot Bridge. Around 11 miles deep at this point and feeling strong. By the BU

Bridge, another water break and the hammies started to tighten. Kept the watch running for a quick stretch and made it to Mass Ave for another pee break. Felt refreshed after the pee and charged into the next few miles. Found community Gatorade around 16th mile which was huge. Felt good around the science museum and had one more water stop/stretch by the boat house. Continued on toward the BU Bridge and broke off to Comm Ave at approximately 18.75 miles. Ran the final 1.25 through Kenmore and up Beacon and once I hit St. Mary's I felt like I'd had enough. Feet/ankles/Achilles were all a bit sore so I thought it was best to stop here rather than push it one more mile. My time was spot on, considering I didn't stop the watch at all to pee, stretch – felt like I had time to play with. Work out the hammies, rest up the body and I should be fine come Oct 22.

DATE	DISTANCE	TIME	COURSE
3-Oct	6x800	3:13-3:19	Brookline Track

NOTES:

Felt all achy during the first few repeats, but probably due to the 20-miler over the weekend and fasting the day before. However, I did hit all 6 repeats under the specified time so I was moving well, just not feeling it. Foot hurt a little bit which has me a bit concerned but just going to rest it over the week and run again on Friday. Cut the repeats from 8 to 6 due to time constraints. Pushed hard on all of them so I felt good leaving the course.

DATE	DISTANCE	TIME	COURSE
6-Oct	13 miles	1:43:32 7:54/pace	Beacon St to Kenmore to Comm Ave to Western Ave to St. Paul to Beacon

NOTES:

Another Friday run – not a huge fan since it throws off my 'clock' but I also knew this would be the last one. Weather was perfect, low 50s and sunny. Last run of any significant distance so I was excited to run it and get it over with. First few miles I felt the usual aches/pains but by mile 6 I was in my groove and felt zoned in from mile 7 til the end. Was able to push it hard the last few miles and finished with a nice sub-8 minute pace. No real pain in the feet/ankles which was a good sign. Taper well the next two weeks and I'm ready to go.

DATE	DISTANCE	TIME	COURSE
10-Oct	5x1K	3:56-4:01	Brookline Track

NOTES:

Was a good 3-6 sec faster than projected times for these repeats. Cut the last one short – did 1 lap instead of 2.5. Pushed hard, felt I was running strong. Legs feel good – gaining confidence as race day nears.

DATE	DISTANCE	TIME	COURSE
12-Oct	6 miles	46:36 7:46/pace	Beacon St – Kenmore Loop

NOTES:

Typical Thursday run for me...my mind was more focused on the weekend and birthday than this run. Almost felt like I just wanted to get it done. Again, body feels good, maintained fast pace – get through Saturday and I'm good to go.

DATE	DISTANCE	TIME	COURSE
15-Oct	8 miles	1:03:41 7:58/pace	Beacon St – Dartmouth Loop

NOTES:

Last run of any distance today. Body felt good. Feels weird not to carb-up in the morning before a run, but 8 miles is nothing right now. Hit my stride at the usual 4-5 mile mark and pretty much cruised to the end of the run. Body scan produced nothing to be concerned with – a good sign. Race is a week away and I'm ready to go!

DATE	DISTANCE	TIME	COURSE
17-Oct	6x400m	1:27-1:31	Brookline Track

NOTES:

Brisk weather, but similar environment to what Chicago should be. Hit all six repeats at or just quicker than 1:30 – which was faster than projected times. Feeling good with less than a week to go. One more training run – feel fresh, legs feel good from massage, no nagging injuries – been a good taper so far.

DATE	DISTANCE	TIME	COURSE
19-Oct	3 miles	22:49 7:31/pace	Beacon St - Coolidge Corner Loop

NOTES:

Quick and easy run. Last one before the race. No pain, feel lean and clean – good diet the past few days. I'm as ready as I'm going to be.

BIBLIOGRAPHY

Crossman, J. (2001). *Coping with Sports Injuries: Psychological strategies for rehabilitation.* New York, NY: Oxford University Press.

Jackson, S.A., and Csikszentmihalyi, M. (1999). *Flow in Sports: The keys to optimal experiences and performance.* Champaign, IL: Human Kinetics.

Pierce, B., Murr, S., and Moss, R. (2007). *Run Less, Run Faster.* New York: Rodale.

Porter, K. (2004). *The Mental Athlete.* Champaign, IL: Human Kinetics.

Stevenson, C.D. and Biddle, S.J. (1998). Cognitive orientations in marathon running and "hitting the wall". *British Journal of Sports Medicine,* 32, 229-234.

Weinberg, R.S., and Gould, D. (2007). *Foundations of Sport and Exercise Psychology (4th ed.).* Champaign, IL: Human Kinetics.

Williams, J.M. (2006). *Applied Sport Psychology: Personal growth to peak performance.* New York: McGraw Hill.

Wilmore, J.H. and Costill, D.L. (1994). *Physiology of Sport & Exercise.* Champaign, IL: Human Kinetics.

LaVergne, TN USA
08 January 2011
211581LV00001B/4/P